st   Ge̶̶̶̶̶̶̶̶̶̶
You
and ♡ P9-BZE-927
and very interesting in
how these Eskimos lived
(SURVIVED) so long ago.

The Winter Walk

The Winter Walk

A Century-old Survival Story from the Arctic

Loretta Outwater Cox

ALASKA NORTHWEST BOOKS®

Anchorage, Alaska ■ Portland, Oregon

Text © 2003 by Loretta Outwater Cox
Photo credits are given with the individual photos.

All rights reserved. No part of this book may be reproduced or transmitted in any
form or by any means, electronic or mechanical, including photocopying, record-
ing, or by any information storage and retrieval system, without written permission
of the publisher.

Library of Congress Cataloging-in-Publication Data

Cox, Loretta Outwater.
   The winter walk : a century-old survival story from the Arctic /
Loretta Outwater Cox.
      p cm.
   ISBN 0-88240-558-6
      1. Qutuuq.   2. Inupiat women—Biography.   3. Inupiat women—Social
   conditions.   4. Inupiat women—Migrations.   5. Inupiat—Social life and
   customs.   I. Title.

   E99.E7Q783   2003
   979.8'60049712—dc21

                                                                    2002155576

Alaska Northwest Books®
An imprint of Graphic Arts Center Publishing Company
P.O. Box 10306, Portland, Oregon 97296-0306
503-226-2402
www.gacpc.com

President: Charles M. Hopkins
Associate Publisher: Douglas A. Pfeiffer
Editorial Staff: Timothy W. Frew, Tricia Brown, Jean Andrews, Kathy Howard,
   Jean Bond-Slaughter
Production Staff: Richard L. Owsiany, Susan Dupere

Editor: Linda Gunnarson
Designer: Elizabeth Watson
Typographer: William H. Brunson Typography Services

Printed in the United States of America

Dedication

To my mother,

Ruth Savok Outwater,

who lived her life teaching,

but only to those who wanted to

watch and listen and learn from her.

She is my greatest teacher.

To my father,

Walter Outwater,

who inspired me to have

the courage of my convictions

and faith in my choices.

You are a good dad.

Contents

Acknowledgments

Thank you to my husband, Skip, our children—Yolanda, Tony, Katherine, and Christopher—and all my relatives for sharing their stories with me, including my Uncle Fred, Aunt Irene, and Aunt Rachel. Thank you to Tricia Brown for discovering the manuscript, for helping it through the process of publication and for believing in it. I'll be forever grateful to my editor, Linda Gunnarson, for turning my thoughts into something readable, to Amelia Nagarak Lovell for finding and sharing Qutuuq's picture, to my mother, Ruth K. Outwater, for all of her help, and to all Iñupiat people who have stories to share and tell.

▰▰▰▰▰▰

Qutuuq designed this unique pattern that was made by sewing small pieces of brown-and-white caribou into a strip. She then sewed the trim onto the flounces of fur parkas or decorated the tops of mukluks *(boots) that she made for her children and grandchildren. The century-old design still identifies Qutuuq's descendants, like a family crest. In the later years, black-and-white calfskin was used.*

Introduction

////////

Listen while I tell you a story.

More than twenty years ago, when I was expecting twins, my mother came to me and told me a story that I'd never heard before. It concerned my great-grandmother, an Iñupiaq woman named Qutuuq, and an extraordinary overland journey toward the Bering Sea coast that Qutuuq made with her two small children in the winter of 1892. The account had been handed down, generation to generation, in our family, and my mother had decided that it was time to give me this story. I would learn about the great danger and the terrible hunger they endured. But more than that, my mother told me the true cost of that long winter walk that began when Qutuuq's son, my grandfather, said, "Mama, I want to live."

—L. O. C.

PRINCIPAL PEOPLE

Qutuuq [COO-took]
An Iñupiaq woman

Kipmalook [kip-MAY-look]
Her husband

Savokġenaq [sav-ga-gee-KNUCK]
Their nine-year-old son

Keenaq [keen-YOCK]
Their seven-year-old daughter

Prologue

///////////

The year was 1921. A five-year-old girl watched as her grandmother, Qutuuq, worked with the bread dough made from hops and boiled rice. The little girl was named Keenaq, after her father's sister. She loved it when her grandmother made bread because she always gave her a little piece of dough to play with and because it smelled so good when the bread was baking. Keenaq is Ruth Savok Outwater, my mother, who told me the story you are about to read.

This story is about an Iñupiat Eskimo family who hunted and gathered different kinds of food, depending on the season. They lived in far northwestern Alaska, on a little spit of land along the Bering Sea, just south of the Arctic Circle, where the winters are long and dark, and the bright summers last long enough to pick greens and berries, dry fish, and maybe enjoy a little warmth from the sun.

As with time immemorial, changes were taking place. At this particular time and place, it was the coming of Western culture. Money could be made, and Qutuuq and her second husband, Okitkun, had an opportunity to open what was called a roadhouse.

The roadhouse became a busy place where travelers, Native and non-Native, stopped to eat or sleep after journeying from another village with a dog team, and where village people dropped by to find out the latest news. Mail carriers stopped there to rest between villages. At that time, Qutuuq's son, Savokġenaq, or John, as he was named by the missionaries, was one of the mail carriers. So, for him, it was like coming home. It was the same for his wife, Lily, his daughter Ruth, and his other children.

The roadhouse was first started at the village of Kuuyuk (Koyuk) but was later moved to a place called Bonanza, which lay between the villages of Kuuyuk and Chaqtuliq (Shaktoolik) on Norton Bay. At Bonanza, the scenery was so beautiful that it could be described as picturesque. On most summer days, one couldn't help but notice the blue-hued mountains nestled beneath an oftentimes blue sky. And on this side of the mountains, the clear Ungalik River flowed, welcoming the many fish that came to feed the Iñupiat people who lived there. Bonanza was also a perfect location for a roadhouse.

Sounds of men working a two-man saw filled the air as they cut driftwood found along the shoreline, to be used for the roadhouse's wood-burning stove. There was much talking and laughing along with the sounds of children and an occasional dog's bark.

When travelers came into the roadhouse, Qutuuq greeted them and made them feel welcome. After her visitors were relaxed, though, she did not sit down and visit for long. Instead, she always got busy with chores that needed to be done.

Qutuuq looked like any of the other grandmas. She wore a parka-style dress of cloth, called a *kuspuk*, and neatly made *mukluks* (boots) of red-dyed seal-skin. She had dark hair that she usually wore in two braids. But it was her eyes that wanted you to hear her stories, and Keenaq loved to sit by her grandma and listen to them.

At the roadhouse, after the meals had been taken care of and the dishes washed, and with fresh ice melting in the pots on the big, black Lang cooking stove, it was usually time for the women of the house to prepare skins for sewing. You could see a sealskin or two soaking in urine behind a stack of wood way off in a back corner of the kitchen. The skins were soaked in urine to make the hair fall out. After a few days, Qutuuq would take the skins out and wash them in another container as many times as needed before they were stretched on a wooden frame and put outside to dry.

Keenaq, who had been named Ruth by Friends Church missionaries, learned how to do this just from watching her grandmother. From Qutuuq, Ruth also learned to make mukluk bottoms by chewing the tough *ugruk* (large bearded seal) hide. Ruth remembers crying because the mukluk bottom would turn out crooked. Qutuuq kept encouraging her, and eventually Ruth learned how to do it right. Many years later, Ruth would make dozens of pairs of mukluks for her own family while they were growing up.

It was during this close time with Qutuuq that Ruth started going to school. Then Ruth's family moved further north to the village of Buckland, where she remembers going to school and crying a lot. It was such a different place, and Ruth felt it would be so much nicer and safer to be home in the roadhouse with Grandma Qutuuq in Bonanza.

Qutuuq and Okitkun ran the roadhouse for a number of years, and Qutuuq cooked, cleaned, and prepared skins for sewing clothes. But as busy as she was, it did not erase from her heart what had happened so long ago, in the year 1892.

Many years earlier, Qutuuq had made up her mind that she wouldn't feel sorry for herself because of what had happened up the river that fateful winter, and would instead focus on her children and, later, her grandchildren. She also knew that her first husband, Kipmalook, her children's father, would have been proud of the life she had lived.

Still, there was this one aspect of this long-ago event that would remain deeply hidden her whole life. Perhaps we can try to understand why if we imagine ourselves back in a time when there were no modern appliances, transportation, or medicines. Imagine if the survival of others as well as ourselves depended on our skills, knowledge, inner strength, and respect.

And so it had been for Qutuuq in 1892.

Determined to Live

◢◤◢◤◢◤◢◤

Qutuuq asked her nine-year-old son, "Savokġenaq, shall we stay here and die like Papa?"

He answered, "No, I don't want to die."

The three of them sat there as Qutuuq held Savokġenaq and his younger sister, Keenaq. They sat for what seemed like an eternity. Only the sounds of their crying and sniffling filled the sod house. The dim flickering of a white tallow candle outlined the body of their papa, Kipmalook. As they sat next to him, Qutuuq whispered to Kipmalook, asking him why he had to get sick and die. What was she supposed to do now? As if waiting for him to answer, she slowly reached over and smoothed his hair back. He had died with his eyes partly open. She thought that perhaps he could see her even in death.

"I asked Savokġenaq if we should die like you," Qutuuq said to him. "We have no more food. Savokġenaq does not want to die. We will have to leave you here."

When she realized what she had said, she started to cry with all the strength she had left.

Savokġenaq held his mother and said, "It'll be okay. We'll make it." Savokġenaq wanted to live, so now he felt that he needed to comfort his mother and Keenaq, who was seven years old.

Qutuuq had known for a long time that Kipmalook was going to die. He had a growth on his neck that had become noticeable to both of them a few months after they arrived at the place they believed was a good hunting ground, a place that was a good distance upriver from their home village of Chaqtuliq on the Bering Sea coast. For a long time, Kipmalook's condition didn't keep him from checking his traps when he could. Then he became very sick.

Although they could see their breath in the sod house, the three were warm because of all the fur pelts gathered around them. They had moved the pelts inside from the storage cache, thinking that they would leave most of them in the sod house with Kipmalook. As if to hold on to their Kipmalook, they all lay down next to him for the last time. Before Qutuuq went to sleep, the baby kicked inside her.

The next morning, Savokġenaq awoke first. When he remembered what had happened, he looked toward

his father and said quietly, "I'm going to take your gun."
He knew Papa was dead, but he still had to ask his permission because that was what Papa had taught him.

As he sat there in the cold, trying to stay still so his
mother would remain asleep, Savokġenaq could barely
make out the long shapes of the willows they had used
to build the sod house. He started to think about that
day when they arrived by the foothills. Papa had all of
them working to gather the long willows to make the
frame for the sod house. Everyone was so happy then.
Savokġenaq pictured in his mind all the food they had,
especially the keg of molasses that he enjoyed so much.
It had come from a trading post at Chaqtuliq, where his
parents bartered fur pelts for food. They also had crackers, tea, and some matches from the trading post.

Savokġenaq reminded himself that now they had no
food, so he shouldn't think about eating. Instead, he
remembered how Papa had told them what to do when
they started building the sod house. They spent the rest
of that warm fall day cutting down willows with a small
axe. Savokġenaq's job was mostly to drag the willows to
the site where they had chosen to build. When Papa
took a break, he would try to work the axe and cut
down willows that were not as thick as the ones Papa
would choose. He and Keenaq would stop sometimes

and eat wild rosehip berries, which were very ripe. His mother would tell them not to eat too many or they would get a stomachache. They also found wild red currant berries, but they preferred the rosehips because they were sweeter.

Once again, Savokġenaq told himself not to think about food because they had none. Papa had been sick for so long that they had run out of everything, and now even the dried meat was gone.

Savokġenaq thought again about how they had built the sod house. When his parents thought they had enough willows, they had stopped working for the first day. With all the willows that they gathered, Kipmalook and Qutuuq made a crude tepee and threw some skins around it for a little protection. It was mostly open to the fresh air since they had only a few skins.

The next day, after eating crackers and berries for breakfast with some tea, they all began working again. Kipmalook used his axe to chop sod from the tundra in rectangular chunks. When the chunks were separated from the ground, Keenaq helped by pulling on them, and it was Savokġenaq's job to carry the sod a few steps to the side.

They started to build on the depression where they had dug up the sod. The shelter would not be too big, about eight feet wide by ten feet long. They dug holes for the four corners and stuck the sturdiest willows there. They placed taller willows in the middle of the eight-foot ends of the shelter. From there, it was easy to tie willows to connect everything. The walls were made by slanting the willows so that the sod would stay on top of them better. The shelter was not very high, just high enough so that Kipmalook could stand. He wasn't a very tall man, maybe five-feet-six or -seven. For a roof, willows were laid side by side, and sod was placed on top of them. They were careful to leave a small hole at the top so that any smoke from their oil lamp would go out.

On their second night at their winter camp, the family slept in their new sod house. Savokġenaq clearly remembered the smell of freshly cut willows and sod. They all liked that smell and said so. Over the door, they hung a large bear skin. That was good enough for now. Later, said Kipmalook, they would have to build an entrance tunnel to keep out the wind.

Qutuug Takes Charge

▰▰▰▰▰▰

As Qutuuq began to stir, Savokġenaq asked her if he should make a fire. Qutuuq said that he should so that they could make hot water for the last of the tundra tea. She told Savokġenaq they had to get ready to leave and still had much left to do.

Savokġenaq went outside to make the fire with dried bark and kindling. They still had a lot of willows because that had been one of Savokġenaq's chores—to make sure there was enough wood to burn. Savokġenaq put the cooking rocks on the fire. This used to be the part Qutuuq enjoyed. She would lie under the fur blankets while the rocks were heating. Then, when they were hot, she would get up and place the hot rocks in the pots made of bark to make hot water.

As all three sat and drank tea, Qutuuq felt stronger because now she had a purpose. When Savokġenaq said that he did not want to die, she knew she had to take charge of her family and get them safely home. She said to Savokġenaq and Keenaq, "We will have good memories of Papa." She reminded them how excited they had been when he first brought home a snowshoe hare, a wolverine, two ptarmigan, and two wolves—all this was from the two-day trapline. First Qutuuq prepared the rabbit and ptarmigan so that they had some meat to cook. Then she helped Kipmalook, who had already started skinning the wolves. She held the skin back as he did the cutting.

Qutuuq loved to listen to Kipmalook's stories about his trips setting the traps and checking them along the trapline. How he would build a little shelter with whatever he could find, mostly chunks of snow, and then eat some dried fish. He would sleep on the one piece of skin he always carried and start back home the next day. Once he told her how one wolf was still alive when he arrived at one of the traps. He was so afraid of the wolf that he almost used the wrong arrow to kill it. By mistake, he had grabbed the arrows used to kill ptarmigan. How Kipmalook had laughed at himself for being so afraid that he didn't think clearly. He believed that the spirit of the wolf would have been insulted if he had used arrows that were made for ptarmigan—that he might not be able to trap a wolf again.

Before Kipmalook got sick, he would go out along his trapline every three or four days. When he stayed home, he and Qutuuq were busy stretching skins, working every day and wondering how much the skins would be worth when they took them to barter at the trading post down in their village of Chaqtuliq.

Kipmalook knew that Qutuuq had come from a rich family. Her father, Anamiaq, had been a great hunter when he was young. They had borrowed his skin boat for this trip upriver before freeze-up and had promised to return it in the spring, when the ice went out after breakup. Going home would be easier since they would float down the river and paddle when necessary to guide the boat.

When Qutuuq was young, her father had given her two blue beads, each the size of a pebble, to make a pair of earrings. She still had the earrings tucked in a little bag made from ermine. On one of their trips north, he had bartered for them with one skin boat and two big bags made of beluga whale stomachs full of *muktuk*, which is the outer layer of the beluga whale that has been dried, cooked, and preserved in its own oil.

Qutuuq smiled as she remembered. When they all finished drinking their hot tea, she said to Savokġenaq and Keenaq, "We will put two wolf skins under Papa and a wolf and wolverine skin to cover him." Once they did that, Qutuuq needed to sit down again because what they did was hard work for a pregnant woman. She told her children to go outside to the cache and pack up two bags of furs—one for Savokġenaq to carry and one for herself.

When Savokġenaq and Keenaq had gone outside, Qutuuq felt that she needed to sit with her husband one last time. As she did, she started to remember how this predicament that she and her children were now in started in the fall, when they had left the village on a winter trapping trip.

The Trip Upriver

//////////

When Kipmalook, Qutuuq, Savokǧenaq, and Keenaq left the village of Chaqtuliq, it was a warm but windy fall day. Qutuuq always preferred the wind because it helped keep the bugs away. Her mother, Icharaq, reminded her to bring along some fungus from dead birch trees, which they could burn to drive away insects as they made their camps along the way up the Chaqtuliq River.

Because she was brought up among good hunters, Qutuuq felt proud as her family set out on their winter trapping trip. She felt proud of Kipmalook because he, too, was a great hunter. They paddled all that first day until it started to get dark. It was easy to fix a meal of boiled fish caught from the river and to whip up some *akutuk*, or Eskimo ice cream, made from caribou fat and salmonberries that she had picked with her mother that summer. In her supplies were also blueberries and blackberries, and she would gather some cranberries along the way or when they reached their destination. Cranberries were not ripe until fall.

The second day, when they stopped to eat, Keenaq started to misbehave because she was tired. She would not eat when told to do so. Qutuuq found two little rocks and began singing to her:

Iglu keta mina ooma mi yu ma,
Akule qutta mina ooma mi yu ma,
Inqiq tal lig mik,
Kilqiq tal lig mik.
If I were a seagull, I would be throwing rocks,
If I were a seagull in a place called Akule,
Where there is a mountain,
Where there is a ptarmigan hawk.

As she sang, Qutuuq juggled the two little rocks in the air. Kipmalook and Savokġenaq both started to chuckle, and it made Keenaq happy, too. She forgot about misbehaving and began to eat.

The river on which the family traveled was full of spawning salmon. They were careful to keep their distance from any brown bears that were eating along the river. Once, when they were paddling, they saw a bear stand up and raise its arms as if to say, "I give up, don't bother me." At that moment, it preferred the fish that were so plentiful to chasing the human beings who were also on the river.

Kipmalook thought to himself, "I'll wait until spring, when you come out of hibernation. Then I'll use the arrow that I'll carve this winter just for bears." He reminded Savokġenaq and Qutuuq to paddle quickly but quietly so they wouldn't attract the bear's attention.

When the family made camp in the evening, they chose the side of the river with fewer willows so that they had a breeze and were safer from any animals that roamed around in the willows. While Qutuuq and Kipmalook set up camp, Savokġenaq and Keenaq explored their surroundings. Once, they ran back to camp out of breath and very much afraid. When Kipmalook asked, "Why did you two run so hard?" they said that while they were looking for muskrats in a lake, two moose suddenly appeared. Savokġenaq said he had never run so hard in his life. At one point he had to go back and take Keenaq's hand since she couldn't keep up with him. It was then that he noticed that the moose were running in the opposite direction. Everyone laughed and laughed. After all the excitement, it was not hard for them all to fall asleep that night.

When they awoke the third day, the sun was shining again. Kipmalook made the fire and placed the rocks so that they would get hot. (They had brought ten nice smooth rocks from the beach by their village for heating water and for cooking.) He thought that it would be a good idea to wash himself in one of the lakes nearby. At the lake's edge, he took off his inner garment, which was made of squirrel skins. As he did so, he could feel a little nip in the air and thought to himself, "I'm so thankful to have a wife who makes me all those warm clothes."

As Kipmalook dove in, making a loud splash and hooting, he woke the children. When he came out, he could see his family watching him and enjoying it because he was being so playful. The three of them decided to go down to the river to wash their hands and their faces. Afterward, breakfast of dried ugruk meat, crackers, and tea was good.

That day they were still a long way from their destination, the place Kipmalook thought would be good for his trapline. They could see the mountains off in the distance. The skies were busy with the movement of ducks, geese, and cranes flying south. Qutuuq loved to watch all the V-shaped formations.

As they paddled, Kipmalook saw some cranes eating berries a little way back from the riverbank. They stopped, and he told Savokġenaq to hold on to the boat as he stood on the riverbank. Then Kipmalook slowly and quietly crawled on the ground until he was close enough to fire his crude gun. He could shoot only once and then had to reload, by which time the birds would fly off. So they repeated this scenario many times, and by late afternoon, they had two geese and two cranes.

While they traveled, Qutuuq plucked and saved all the feathers. Keenaq tried to pluck too. Qutuuq felt good watching her. She remembered that that was the way she had learned—by watching her mother and doing what she did. Qutuuq had learned to pluck the feathers very fast because, when she was little, a *qumaq* (a bug from the duck) started to crawl up her arm. She knew that the faster she plucked, the faster the work would be done. The thought always made her laugh.

Qutuuq's bottom teeth were worn down because she had also learned to be a good skin-sewer and could make mukluks like her mother. She had practiced over and over again, chewing on ugruk soles. The procedure was to crimp the front and the back of the ugruk piece. If you were not good at it, your family would end up wearing crooked mukluks, and that would be embarrassing. She knew that was how she was going to teach Keenaq: by having her watch first, and then, when she felt she was ready to try, she would tell her mother. That way Keenaq would not be forced to do something and then ridiculed by other skin-sewers if it did not turn out right.

Qutuuq's mother had first taught her how to make simpler items of clothing such as fur mittens and fur socks. Qutuuq remembered being eleven years old and asking her mom for help sewing because it was too hard for her. Qutuuq promised herself that when the time came to teach her own daughter, she would try to have as much patience as her mother had had with her. By the time she was fourteen, Qutuuq had become a very good seamstress and helped make any clothing the family needed.

As they made camp for the third night, Qutuuq prepared some goose soup, and it was delicious. She had put in some wild onions, which were plentiful everywhere. Kipmalook was given the best part of the goose, the breast. Qutuuq liked the back part and everything that was connected to it. They both loved to sit and eat every bit of meat off the bones. The children ate the legs and wings. Because he was a boy, Savokġenaq also got the head. He had learned to open the skull and enjoy the delicacy of the meat there, along with the eyeballs and the tongue. He felt special when something was meant only for him because he was the boy.

It had been a busy day. Everyone was tired but content by bedtime.

As they started out again the next day, Kipmalook told his family that they should make as much headway as possible that morning. The river seemed very long because there were so many bends. They watched the sky for any change in the weather. So far, there were no rain clouds, for which they were grateful. If it did rain, though, they were prepared for it. During the previous winter, when they had planned this trip, Qutuuq worked diligently on the intestines of the ugruk seals. She spent hours carefully cutting them open so they could be stretched and dried. She and her mother then made rain gear by sewing all the long strips of intestines into raincoats. Her mother told her that the rain gear would last for many years and would still be useful for her grandchildren.

As they traveled farther inland, the river became shallower. They could see every fish in the river when it wasn't reflecting the sun. As they came to a huge school of arctic char, Kipmalook could not pass them up. He loved the taste of aged white fish. During the winter they would eat the fish partially thawed. The eggs and the liver were the most delicious part of the fish. They were always a treat.

Kipmalook got out his little net made from sinew. The net measured about six feet long. Every time Kipmalook set it out, he pulled in fish right away. The children laughed and had fun trying to catch any fish that tried to swim away as Kipmalook threw them up on the ground. When there was a pile of fish, Kipmalook thought they had enough.

"Now, what are we going to do with all these fish?" Kipmalook playfully asked his wife.

When they decided to make a fire and have lunch, Qutuuq suggested that they dig a hole in the ground and leave most of the fish behind to age instead of taking them all with them. Everyone helped dig the hole while the rocks were getting hot to make tea. It was the children's job to carry rocks from the riverbed to mark the site so that Kipmalook would be able to find it even under the snow in three or four months.

After all that digging, the family decided to eat a light lunch of dried meat dipped in seal oil and some fresh blackberries with a smattering of blueberries mixed in to sweeten the mix. Qutuuq was careful not to eat blackberries if times were stressful. It was fine now because everything was running smoothly. She believed that the blackberries had a stronger spirit than blueberries because they grew closer to the ground. Like her parents, she, too, believed that everything had a spirit—animals, plants, even hills. They also believed it was important to leave behind a little of whatever they were gathering or hunting to say thank you, so that they would continue to have plenty.

When they resumed their journey again, Qutuuq sat quietly admiring her husband. She knew that she had a part in helping him, but he was such a hard worker and took great pride in his family. He was a kind and caring person who loved his children and his wife. Qutuuq felt fortunate that their parents— hers and his—had matched them to become husband and wife.

Kipmalook's parents were shamans. Their names were Kalineq and Utuktak. Qutuuq knew that they had performed a ritual that was supposed to pass on shamanic power to Savokġenaq. He must have been a toddler because they had to carry him on their backs whenever it had taken place. For a long time, Savokġenaq carried a little charm—a dried-up little squirrel. Qutuuq never believed in shamanic powers because when she was little, a shaman told the children to shut their eyes so they wouldn't see a spirit. She was curious and peeked. When she opened her eyes a crack, she didn't see anything. When they were back home in Chaqtuliq, away from the presence of her in-laws, she would tell Savokġenaq not to believe what was said to him. Qutuuq knew that respect for elders was a rule that everyone lived by, but she also knew that pretending not to hear an elder was accepted and therefore not a sign of disrespect.

As they traveled now, the foothills were closer. They were getting anxious to reach their destination, the place where the river flowed swift and shallow. Kipmalook encouraged them and kept them paddling on the river long into the evening. The river was shallow in some places, and it was necessary for three of them to jump out and pull and push the skin boat. Keenaq remained in the boat because she was little. They all wore waterproof mukluks that Qutuuq and her mother had made the winter before. The sound they made while pushing against the water was entertaining to Keenaq.

Because of the shallowness of the river, they had to pull the boat every few yards. They were concentrating so hard that they forgot to stop and eat. When Keenaq told them she was hungry, Qutuuq quickly found the bag that contained dried caribou meat. As they pulled, Keenaq rode and chewed on the dried meat. Pretty soon Savokġenaq wanted to eat, so he jumped back in the boat, too.

The two children started to play a game they called "muck." They would both say the word and then stare at each other to see who would laugh first. The one who laughed first was the loser. Savokġenaq was always the loser; he always seemed to see something funny on his sister's face. Keenaq liked winning because Savokġenaq always got to do more things because he was older.

After a while, the adults pulled the skin boat up on a sandbar that looked like a good place to rest. Everyone helped gather dried sticks to use as firewood. They were so tired that Kipmalook thought it might be good to make camp for the night. They brought ashore two caribou skins and lay down on them. Qutuuq went back to the boat for some of the birch fungus to smoke on the fire to drive off the gnats that were flying about. It felt good to the family to lie there and rest, for they had worked harder that day than any other day on the river.

That night, they took their time preparing a dinner of one of the cranes that Kipmalook had shot. He looked for two sturdy sticks, sharpened the ends, and stuck them through the crane; then he braced them at an angle with the meat closest to the fire. Once in a while, he would turn the sticks to cook the other side of the crane meat. While they were waiting for the crane to cook, Qutuuq cut some dried caribou meat and fat. They snacked on that with crackers and tea. She also took out some willow greens, called *serra*, that she had preserved in seal oil. Tonight the food tasted extra good because they had worked up such a big appetite pulling the boat through the shallow water.

After dinner, Savokġenaq and Keenaq explored the sandbar as their parents sat and watched them. Qutuuq and Kipmalook were very proud of how the children got along with each other. Savokġenaq took care of his sister, and Keenaq listened when he told her to do something. That evening, Kipmalook and Qutuuq's conversation was about having another baby. That was when Qutuuq told her husband that she felt she was already pregnant. They talked about who the third baby would be like—Savokġenaq or Keenaq. Or maybe the baby would just have his or her own personality. That gave them something to look forward to in the future.

Remembering a Trip Up North

///////////

Qutuuq's thoughts returned to the present and to the journey back to their village. She looked around in the little sod house to make sure that she wouldn't forget anything. It was so hard to get up now that she was in her seventh month of pregnancy. She tried not to complain because she and Kipmalook had wanted this baby. She checked the place where she kept her special things and found the blue beads that had been made into earrings. They were a treasured possession, and she could not leave them behind. She held them in her hands and remembered the time when her parents had given them to her.

Qutuuq remembered that her family had traveled north for two summers in a skin boat in the Bering Sea. The first village they had reached was Kuuyuk, which was situated on a bay, set back on the edge of a grove of spruce trees. The dwellings were made with spruce logs that were split in half and covered with sod. The people there had interesting stories to tell about their battles with the Indians that would come from inland to steal women to take back as wives. In their language the Indians were called *Inukquotuks.*

The residents also told them that, in the spring, the young people would gather down by the river, make a fire, and tell stories. Sometimes, they would play a game called *mana mana*, in which they chose two teams. The goal was to run around the opposite base without being tagged. Once in a while, someone would run as far as a mile to try to score a point. If a person did get tagged, he or she would go to a holding circle just opposite the base.

It was fun there at Kuuyuk. That was also where she saw a lot of poles sticking out of the mud down at the bay. They held fishing nets in place. Once she went down with the family of one of her friends at low tide, when they could see the fish hanging on the nets. They caught salmon, trout, and lingcod. When the weather was nice, the women celebrated the catch by making a feast down by the shore. Fresh greens from the beach were put into a pot along with fish, to be eaten by anyone who was hungry after the hard work of harvesting food from the bay.

It was at Kuuyuk that Qutuuq's father, Anamiaq, hunted belugas with the men of the village. They were skilled in using the harpoon to hunt the whales. As many as six or seven could be put away to be shared by the whole village. Qutuuq and the other girls her age helped cut the muktuk into rectangular pieces that were all connected at the corners and then hung to dry on racks for a few days. Then the muktuk was cooked in hot water in huge outdoor containers acquired from the trading post.

Some of the muktuk was stored away without being cooked. The whales' flippers were cut into strips and stored to age. The stomachs were cleaned and blown up like balloons to be used as containers.

As with the fish-harvest feasts, some of the beluga meat was also cooked daily, and anyone could help themselves when they got hungry. Most of it was cut into strips for dried jerky.

Because Anamiaq was a good hunter, the village had given him two beluga stomachs full of muktuk to take with him as the family continued its journey north.

During their stay at Kuuyuk, Qutuuq and her family had been the guests of Kalineq and Utuktak, who, as shamans, were highly respected in the village. When it came time to continue on their journey north, both sets of parents had agreed that Qutuuq and Kipmalook would be married when they came of age. Qutuuq just shrugged her shoulders when her parents told her. At that age, she had other things to think about.

When the family arrived at Nook (Teller), the residents there were catching salmon, so they decided to stay about two weeks to dry some fish for the winter. Anamiaq and Icharaq were a hardworking team, and people knew that Anamiaq was a good hunter and provider. They also believed that Anamiaq had good luck when he hunted or fished.

As they helped cut and dry fish, Icharaq cut a few of the fish and left the eggs inside to prepare an exotic dish. It would be eaten after it had aged. At this time, Qutuuq did not care for the aged eggs. She remembered plugging her nose and wondering, "How can they eat that stuff?"

The young children's job was to gather wood and willows to help create the smoke that kept blue flies away from the drying fish. It was important to create smoke constantly for three or four days until the fish were half dry so that the blue flies couldn't lay their eggs on them. When the family was ready to leave, they had a bundle of dried fish to sustain them for the rest of the summer and into the winter.

At times, the ocean was too rough to travel, but when they could, they paddled long days trying to reach their next destination—this time, a village to the west called Kiŋigin (Wales). On Anamiaq's previous trips, he had become close with a family in that village. He knew that they would be stopping there for a few days and that it was the best place to barter for ivory, skin boats, and walrus hides.

When they reached Kiŋigin, everyone was happy to see them. Anamiaq's friend was also a great hunter and was thought to be wealthy. This time, Anamiaq bartered all his spear points for one skin boat and some walrus hides. It had been worth it to spend all that time carving extra ones to barter. Their friends also wanted to make the trip to Qikiqtaġruk (Kotzebue), the village up north, so now there would be two boats traveling together. They wanted to trade ivory and walrus *quoke*—the cooked outer skin of the walrus—for some black muktuk brought by the Iñupiat people from above Qikiqtaġruk.

This trip was different because the Iñupiat talked of others who came from across the ocean to the west. The new traders were also Native people. So instead of bartering for foods from farther up north, they were awed by the new traders' colorful beads and began bartering for them.

Anamiaq saw how Icharaq looked at the beads. He thought to himself and then said to his wife, "We can afford two beads for Qutuuq's ears. The trader said that they could be bartered for one skin boat and two stomachs of white muktuk."

Icharaq chuckled because she was so happy, and that's the way Qutuuq came to own two blue beads, each the size of a pebble.

That year, Qutuuq remembered, they had spent the winter up north because it was too late to make it back all the way home before freeze-up. At spring breakup, they headed back, hunting and fishing along the way.

Preparing to Leave

Just then, as Qutuuq tucked away her blue beads and the memories they held, Savokġenaq and Keenaq walked in. Normally, they were noisy children, but today Qutuuq hardly heard them. Savokġenaq told her that he had packed two bags of skins. While he and Keenaq were packing the skins, Keenaq had found a piece of dried meat that had fallen in with them. It was enough for two meals and had a little fat on it, which was good. Savokġenaq said that he also found some tea that they had picked off the tundra last fall.

Qutuuq started to cry softly as she thought about leaving, but then told herself that she had better decide what to do next. She said to her children, "We will bring Papa to the cache and that's where we will leave him."

Savokġenaq and Keenaq helped their mother drag Kipmalook out on the skins he was lying on. He was heavy, and they would tug and stop, tug and stop. When they had finally pulled Kipmalook through the long entryway and made it to the outdoors, Qutuuq started to cry again. She was so sad that he couldn't go on out by himself anymore. Soon the children were crying because Qutuuq was crying so hard.

After a time, Qutuuq started to talk to Kipmalook. "I have known you since you were a young boy. You were named after your grandpa, and people said that you were just like him. You go and find him now and see if you are like him."

Qutuuq believed that there was a Great Maker of all things, and she asked Him now to help them on their journey back to their village.

"Kipmalook, thank you for being the good provider when you were with us. You were a good father and my good husband," she said and then started to cry again. Only when Keenaq tugged at her did she realize that they should keep pulling him toward the storage cache.

When they reached the cache, Qutuuq said that Savokġenaq should go back inside the sod house and get the skins they had used when they thought they were going to leave his papa there.

When Savokġenaq came back with the skins, she had him climb up on the cache, which was about four feet off the ground. She handed him the skins, which he laid on the floor of the cache. Then she told him to come back down so that they could both lift Kipmalook up. Savokġenaq would have to pull from inside once they lifted him to the doorway because Qutuuq was too large in her pregnancy.

When they finally got Kipmalook in the right place, she asked Savokġenaq if he could touch him once more on the cheek for her and for Keenaq and for himself and say, "Good-bye, Papa." Then she handed Savokġenaq the skins to cover Kipmalook as the tears rolled silently down her cheeks.

When they were finished and started walking back toward the sod house, Qutuuq asked Savokġenaq again, "Savokġenaq, do you still want to live? Or shall we stay here and die like Papa?"

It frightened Savokġenaq to hear his mother ask him again, so he pleaded with her that they should live. And again she said, "Okay, we will live."

Before they went back inside the sod house, Qutuuq asked Savokġenaq to fix the fire and put the heating rocks on while she cut up the meat that Keenaq had found. When the fire was burning hot, they warmed their hands and went back into the sod house.

Qutuuq told both her children to come and sit with her while they chewed on the dried meat and fat. As they sat there, she told them that they would start to walk back to the village the next morning. Two bags of fur were ready, and she just needed to check a few more places in their little sod house so she wouldn't leave anything important behind.

"We will need to rest all we can today," she told her children.

They sat and chewed a long time; then the heating rocks were ready to make hot water, and they drank some tea. No one felt like talking much. They just sat and thought about what they had just done. The children wanted to go out and play when they were through having tea, leaving Qutuuq to her own thoughts, which turned to the cache where her husband now lay.

That fall, after they had built the sod house, Kipmalook wanted to make a cache to store all the furs he would be getting after freeze-up. They also needed a place to store all the dried meat and dried fish, and all the berries, greens, and seal oil.

First, they made four holes and dug out a rectangular space to about four feet by six feet. Just doing that took them the whole day. Qutuuq also stacked some of the moss that they had dug up. This would be used as toilet paper in the outhouse and as diapers for the new baby. That day, when they stopped working for a while, Kipmalook suggested that they explore around their sod house.

As they were walking among the birch trees, they came to a stream that ran into the main river. There they found a family of beavers busily getting ready for the winter, just as they were. They sat and watched them work. When the sun was getting low on the horizon, it was time to head back to their own place. When they got back, Qutuuq made a dinner of dried fish, seal oil, serra, white muktuk, salmonberries, and tea. That combination was usually their main meal. After dinner, everyone went outside and did end-of-the-day chores: getting some water, chopping a few pieces of wood for the morning, and making sure everything was put inside the sod house just in case it rained during the night. Kipmalook could tell by looking at the clouds if it was going to rain. He said that it would rain for sure in two days.

The next day they chopped down four fat birch trees to be used for vertical corner poles on the cache. This took the whole morning. They made four pieces, each about eleven feet long, and put them into the holes that they had dug the day before.

The foundation of the cache was made of two willows secured with ugruk rawhide on notches cut into the vertical poles about five feet off the ground. On top of these two pieces they laid the floor of small birch trees that were about four inches thick. To put up the walls, three- or four-inch willows were secured in the notches using ugruk rawhide. Kipmalook decided to make the roof flat because it was just for their furs and food storage—a place to keep food cool in the fall and out of reach of animals such as wolves and foxes. On the top, they laid chunks of sod over the willows.

It had been another hard day's work, and they were proud of it. They did not know that someday the cache would be used as a grave.

Settling into the Sod House

///////////

Just then, Savokġenaq and Keenaq came back inside to warm up a little, interrupting Qutuuq's reverie. Savokġenaq asked his mother if she was all right. Qutuuq said that she was, just tired. She told him she wanted to sit a while longer to rest for the long journey home. Savokġenaq said they only came in to check on her and wanted to play outside a while longer. Qutuuq told them not to go far and that they all would be going to bed early that night. Then she closed her eyes and remembered back once more.

Kipmalook was right. It did rain the following day. He said that he had learned from his uncle how to tell when it was going to rain, by watching what kind of clouds were in the sky. To be a good hunter, his uncle had told him, it was important to learn the weather signs so he wouldn't lose his catch or be stranded somewhere.

Kipmalook's father, Kalineq, was a spiritual man, and from him he learned that all animals had spirits. Animals were proud of what they were, and that is why he taught Kipmalook to respect them and to be sure to use the right arrows for each animal.

When Kipmalook was getting ready for this trip, he left at home all the arrows used to hunt seals and other ocean animals. He took with him only the arrows made for inland animals: one for the wolf, and smaller ones for the ptarmigan and the rabbit. He knew that he had lots of time to make one for the bear he would be hunting in the spring, when bears came out of hibernation.

It rained for five days. The fall rains were cold, and it was hard to keep up with drying out the firewood. Kipmalook told his family that one of the things they would do next, as soon as the rain stopped, was to gather a pile of firewood as tall as their sod house.

The family had to stay in most of the time now. This was when Qutuuq unpacked her oil lamp made of rock. She said they would save the tallow candles for emergency use just in case they ran out of seal oil. The warm glow from the oil lamp always made her feel warm inside. She loved the smell of the burning wick. It made her think of her parents' home.

As they began to settle into their new sod house, each of them picked out a favorite spot. Qutuuq's was between the oil lamp and the place where they ate. Kipmalook liked to sit on the other side of the place where they ate and by the entryway. Savokġenaq's spot was next to his father, and little Keenaq liked to sit by her mother.

After meals were over, Qutuuq worked on stretching and softening the squirrel skins that she brought. There were about forty of them. It took her a whole day to soften one skin, but that was all right because she would have a lot of time to work on them. Eventually, Qutuuq would make each member of her family a new undergarment. As she worked, she and Kipmalook told stories about camping out in the spring to hunt squirrels. How delicious the squirrels were to eat! They would laugh as they remembered some funny thing that had happened. On one such occasion, Kipmalook decided to carve Qutuuq some new needles because, he told her, her needs came first since she made all their clothing items. If she didn't sew, the family would be cold, especially during the winter months.

As Qutuuq sat there remembering, she started to cry as she recalled those words. Kipmalook always made her feel that she was the most important person to him. He was never mean, like some other husbands. Now she had no husband, no one to talk to about raising their children. What about the baby inside her? What would his or her name be? They never talked about that because Kipmalook was so sick the last two months. This time, she was crying for herself, not for Kipmalook.

She didn't know how long she sat there. When she realized that the children were still outside, she made herself go out and check on them. It was so hard to crawl out the entryway now. Once outside, she went to check the skin flap that was the door to the cache where Kipmalook lay. To make sure that wild animals would not get to him, she cut two holes at the bottom of the flap and tied it to the willows that the cache was made of. Qutuuq breathed hard as she did this, and she started to cry again. When she was done, she said, "There, I can leave you."

Then Qutuuq sat down for a while and noticed that it was still early in the evening. She heard the children down by the river at their favorite spot. Walking over to them, she sat down and told them to keep sliding down the riverbank, that they still had time to play. As she sat there on the snow, she looked across the river, recalling again their first days at the sod house.

After it had rained for about five days, Kipmalook told them that they had to do two things before freeze-up. He wanted to work on their woodpile and then take one whole day to boat across the river and walk upriver about a mile. They would look for the edible roots of the wild potato, which should be plentiful now. The food could be eaten raw or cooked. It would be stored in seal oil to preserve it. To find it, they all had to look for what was by then a dried-up bunch of plants with tops that looked like a slingshot. Once they were on their walk and shown what to look for, the children were the ones running around and finding the plants.

Kipmalook and Qutuuq each used their *siqlaq*—a homemade tool, like a pick—to dig the roots from the ground. Savokġenaq and Keenaq ran down to the river to wash some for everyone to eat as they dug them out of the ground. It was so much fun that day. It was hard work, but it was gratifying, especially when they found large roots.

They stopped working to have lunch, which was usually their main meal, but the treat for the children that day was molasses. Qutuuq surprised the children with it every once in a while. It was only for special occasions, and Savokġenaq loved to dip his crackers in it.

After they rested for a while, Kipmalook wanted to climb a small rocky knoll to scout for moose for the next trip upriver. He wanted to pick out the best place to boat to and hunt.

As they started up the knoll, Kipmalook told them to be quiet at first, because wild animals might be in the dense areas. They all walked together, moving in single file through the deep bushes. As they helped each other hold branches back, Qutuuq had a habit of checking out the greens that grew under the tall willows. She noticed that there were *qutlerucks* that were almost dead now. Qutlerucks had round leaves with crimped edges, and Qutuuq would pick them in the spring and mix them in with the serra leaves that she also picked when they were just starting to grow. She also noticed ferns everywhere. They liked to eat ferns when they just started growing too; they looked like little squirrels standing up.

It smelled like a large animal had walked where the family was climbing. It was probably a moose because moose droppings were here and there. When they finally got out of the tall bushes, Keenaq was so relieved that she forgot about being quiet and exclaimed, "Whew, that was some walk!"

They all laughed, and Qutuuq told Keenaq that she had walked through the bushes just like a grown-up.

Now that they were out in the open on a little slope, it was all right to relax and talk since that they could see that there were no wild animals around.

As the family continued to walk up the slope, Qutuuq found cranberries that she wanted to pick and put away for the winter. She told her family to go ahead and walk farther up the hill while she stayed to gather the berries. She picked for about three hours while her family was scouting for moose. She felt safe because she knew that Kipmalook was watching out for her. By the time the three of them came back down, she had a skin pack about three-fourths full of cranberries, and her birch basket was almost full again. When they got back down to the site where they had dug for wild potato roots, they just rested there without looking around for more, because they were getting tired and still had to paddle back down to their camp.

The next day, when the family awoke, they felt tired from having done so much work the day before. Kipmalook suggested they should just rest that morning. When the weather was nice, as it was that day, they lived outside. A few feet from the sod house toward the river they had set up a place where they made a fire to cook. If they weren't cooking or heating rocks to make hot water, they used the outside fire to help keep bugs away, smoldering the fungus growth from dead birch trees. They always took out two caribou skins to sit on.

The day was beautiful. Looking north, they could see the foothills across the river through an opening in the birch trees. That morning, the children skipped rocks in the river, tried to climb some trees, and played hide-and-seek.

Kipmalook and Qutuuq mostly sat and planned what they needed to do. Kipmalook told his wife stories about when he was a young boy. In the fall, his family would get out their bird net, which was quite long. It had taken them several days to make it by hand out of sinew. Kipmalook and his father would go up on the hill behind the village, secure both ends of the net down, and then tie one long pole in the middle of the net. When he was just learning how to do that, Kipmalook would stay by his father at the middle of the net. When a flock of ptarmigan came their way, they would be very still and quiet, almost lying on the ground. Their fur clothes were the same color as the ground, so it would look like there was no one around. Just when the flock flew over them, they quickly jerked the net off the ground with the long pole, catching as many as a dozen birds at a time. Kipmalook told

Qutuuq that hunting those birds was one of his favorite childhood memories.

Kipmalook also told her that when he was a young boy, he didn't think anything of his father being a shaman. His father treated him like all the other fathers treated their sons. It was only later, when he became a teenager, that he realized what his father was. He and his mother, Utuktak, would be called to people's houses when someone got sick, and they always tried to heal them. He knew that they carried a skin bag with mixtures and other things, such as dried-up animal skins. He told Qutuuq he never saw what his parents did to help a sick person. They always told him not to go with them. They had realized when Kipmalook was young that they did not want to pass on their shaman's role to him. But years later they tried to pass their powers on to Savokġenaq, their grandson, which Qutuuq and Kipmalook did not approve of. Just then, the couple looked at each other and realized that they worked well as a team, especially when it came to protecting their children.

A Good Place

////////

Now, as Qutuuq sat watching Savokġenaq and Keenaq slide down the riverbank, she told herself that she would still be their protector, just as when Kipmalook was alive. She looked at the sun and knew it was almost dark. She told her children that they all better get ready for bed now. They would make a fire and hot tea and eat the last of the dried meat for the night. It would be a long day when they started walking back to the village. As they went back to the sod house, she told Savokġenaq and Keenaq to use the outhouse, put away their sliding skins, and take some wood into the dwelling. When she got to the entryway, she started to remember back to the fall, when they had all worked together on it.

It had been that afternoon after they had rested all morning. Kipmalook had everyone working again. After cutting down a large birch tree, he cut the tree in half. Each piece was about eight feet long. They laid the two pieces down facing southeast. Kipmalook said they shouldn't be facing north or east because of the bad winds from those two directions. The west winds were cold also. Then they cut down some long, skinny willows and tied each end down on both sides of the birch logs on the ground. They did this with as many as twenty willows. When that was done, they had interwoven the ugruk rawhide through the willows. This made the entryway very sturdy. Because it was made low to keep out those winter winds, all of them had to stoop down a little bit when using it.

The next day, the family had worked all day cutting sod to stack over the entryway. It was roomy enough so that firewood could be stacked there, a good place for food that would be eaten that week, and also a good storage place for skins that they were working on. When it was done, Kipmalook asked Qutuuq to cut some holes on two sides of a bear skin. Then he fastened the top and one side down to the entryway. Now, they had finished building a warm sod house, a good place to spend that winter.

Qutuuq smiled at the memory of their accomplishment. When they all got back inside, Qutuuq told Savokġenaq to go out and make the fire as she started cutting the meat to eat for their last meal there. As they ate, she told them not to worry about walking back down to the village, that they would make it. The two children listened. Savokġenaq knew that his mother was worried, that maybe she was trying to convince herself. He hadn't thought about the journey until now, about whether or not they would make it. He was sad only when they would cry for their papa. Then he would forget for a while and want to play.

After they had eaten and drunk the last of the tundra tea, they went to bed. But Qutuuq couldn't sleep. She thought once more of all the happy times spent with Kipmalook at the sod house, remembering all that had happened during those months.

Last fall, when they paddled up the river the last time, Kipmalook shot a moose with his long gun. Usually, he preferred hunting with his bow and arrows, but this time he wanted to make use of the gun that he had bartered for at the trading post down in Chaqtuliq. It had cost him ten furs, which was expensive. He had learned to sneak up on his prey for hours before he would shoot the gun. He had just one chance because it took so long to reload.

When Kipmalook had climbed the little hill three weeks earlier, he had learned where the moose were.

This time, it was harder to see them because they blended in so well with the fall colors. But he blended in, too, with his fur clothes. He kept his hood on and hid the gun under a piece of caribou skin. Before he started toward the moose, he made sure that he was upwind from them so they would not smell him. He shot one and hollered to his family, who were waiting by the boat about a quarter of a mile away. They all were happy and relieved that they could stop being so quiet now.

When the children reached their papa, he was already cutting up the moose. He had the moose antlers off and the head removed. When Qutuuq got there, he had the stomach cut open and was saving some blood in a pouch made from waterproof sealskin. He would use this later out on the trapline. He told Qutuuq to hold the skin back while he cut it off. They would be tanning the skin later, so he was careful not to put a hole in it.

After the skin was off, about two hours later, it was time for lunch. They knew it would take them the rest of the day to pack all the meat down to the boat, so they took a long lunch break and rested. Qutuuq took the time to thank the spirit of the moose for allowing them to kill it for their food and clothing. She said that they would not waste anything. As she talked, her husband and children sat and listened. She knew what to do because she had watched her mother perform this ceremony many times. When she was through, she told everyone, "Let's get back to work!"

The family worked hard hauling all of the moose meat to their boat and finally set off paddling. They got home to the sod house around midnight. They all were so tired that they just washed and went to bed.

The next morning, they took their time getting up because they knew they had to work on the moose meat and take care of the hide. Qutuuq made a breakfast of crackers, dried meat, and hot tundra tea. They started to work on the meat about mid-morning. As Qutuuq started slicing the meat to dry, Kipmalook went out to get some willows to make a drying rack. It would extend out from the food cache, so he had to dig only two holes this time. Savokġenaq cut down some skinny willows to hang the meat on; he was beginning to be a big help now. Keenaq sat by her mother and watched her. She was still too young to work with the *ulu*, the women's knife.

They had already taken care of the heart and liver by cutting them into pieces to boil for eating in the next few days. It was still not freezing cold, so they could not freeze any of the meat yet; therefore everything was cut up to dry, even the ribs. As she cleaned out the stomach, Keenaq plugged her nose, which made her mom laugh. She had just found some partially digested willow and lake greens. Qutuuq told her daughter that they didn't eat what was in the moose's stomach, but later on, when Papa killed a caribou, the stomach contents could be eaten. Again, Keenaq made a funny face because the thought of eating what was in a caribou's stomach didn't sound very good.

Qutuuq wanted to make a container out of the stomach, so she carefully cleaned it so that it could be dried. She told Keenaq to go inside the sod house to get her needle and sinew to sew the bottom of the stomach.

Qutuuq was through by the time Kipmalook and Savokġenaq finished the drying rack. They stopped just long enough to stoke the fire, putting some more wood on it to burn hot. They put on the heating rocks, and then everyone kept working to hang all the meat. Qutuuq started cooking the heart and liver pieces while Kipmalook kept on working. The children needed to stop and just watch now. Later, it felt good to sit down and eat a dinner of liver and heart dipped in seal oil with hot broth to drink. Qutuuq stored what was left of the cooked liver and heart in a container with some serra. Working with the head and the hooves would take another two days of effort.

Every day, for about the next two weeks, they spent right at the sod house. They kept the fire smoldering under the meat because, even though it was close to freeze-up time, there were still a few blue flies. Kipmalook and Qutuuq worked on skinning the moose head. It took all day to cook the head once they had skinned it. The first meal from the head was eating the meat from it. Then Qutuuq and Kipmalook loved to sit and chew on the bones from the head for a long time.

The rest of the head was eaten as a side dish to add variety to whatever else they were having. They decided to store the hooves in the food cache for the time being. Later, they would cook the hooves and make a gelatin meatloaf. In this meatloaf, Qutuuq would put some of the liver and heart and serra that she had stored away.

By this time, it had been about two months since they had come up the river. They kept time with the cycles of the moon. Kipmalook kept track by carving little notches on a piece of driftwood he took with him the month they began traveling upriver.

Every day it was getting colder. With the chilling north wind and snow, the river was freezing. This was the time of year Kipmalook was waiting for so that he could begin his trapping. As they waited, the whole family spent each day chopping and hauling willows for firewood. At the end of three weeks the woodpile was as high as the sod house.

They also gathered dried birch bark to use as kindling and a certain willow that they would need for medicinal purposes. This willow was about four feet high and was found right alongside the river. Qutuuq used it for pain when she had her menstrual period before she became pregnant or when someone was getting a bad cold. It also helped relieve headaches and fevers. Qutuuq also collected some stinkweed. She picked about four bundles, tied their stems with rawhide, and had Kipmalook hang them from the ceiling in the food cache. Stinkweed was prepared as a paste and applied to any pain on the body; or if a strong medicine was needed for a bad cold, a liquid was made from its leaves and the sick person would drink this very potent concoction. Sometimes it worked, but not every time.

As the family watched the river freeze day by day, Qutuuq started to spend more of her time indoors. She took care of the daily meals, Savokġenaq made sure the woodpile was piled high with wood, and Keenaq helped her brother. Although it was cold, the children were still able to play outdoors because of their warm clothing. Qutuuq knew that before the winter was over, they all would need new undergarments, and she often sat softening the squirrel skins she brought with her. It would take about a month to finish that project.

While she was doing this, Kipmalook worked outside making skin stretchers out of willow. He had ten traps that he had bartered for from the trading post, so he was busy making ten fur stretchers. From experience he could estimate about how large a wolf, wolverine, lynx, fox, or snowshoe hare would be when the skin was stretched out. He also made one huge one for the moose skin that would be stretched soon. Right now they had the moose hide inside the entryway, where it was warm, so that they could work on it. This large stretcher would also be used for a bear skin in the spring. Kipmalook slowly curved the ends on each skin frame so that they could be connected by tying them with rawhide.

Savokġenaq was a big help connecting the ends together. He loved to work when his papa asked him to. He was excited when Kipmalook told him that he would be taking him out on the short trapline. He would be setting traps over a short distance that could be traveled in one day. This line would head toward the place downriver where they had buried the white fish. Walking on the frozen river and then taking shortcuts on the land would make the distance shorter than it would be if they walked only on the winding frozen river. Kipmalook told Savokġenaq that maybe next year, when he turned ten, he would be ready to go with him on the two-day trapline.

Savŏkgenag's Training Begins

//////////////

During those months, after the evening meal was eaten, when they were too tired to sew or carve, the family spent the time singing and dancing. Kipmalook would beat the drum and the three would dance, or Qutuuq would beat the drum and the rest would dance. They sang and danced all the dances that they had learned from their families and from people back at the village.

One evening, Qutuuq told her family that they should work on a new song and dance so that when they went back to the village, they could perform it in front of the village people, telling them a story of their trip. These were the words to their song:

Naṅgiaqtuq, awshega,
Naṅgiaqtuq, awshega.
Amaġuq,
Qavvik,

Ukalliq,
Kayuqtuq,
Quyana, quyana.
It's good to be trapping,
It's good to be trapping.
Wolf,
Wolverine,
Red fox,
Rabbit,
Thank you, thank you.

Qutuuq wanted to let the villagers know how successful they were in preparing and preserving all the food from plants and animals. And soon Kipmalook would be trapping animals for their furs. She told Kipmalook that while he was out walking the trapline he should make up the words for a song and dance about trapping. He told her that he would.

Finally, the day came for Qutuuq to prepare food for Kipmalook because the weather conditions were right for trapping. The river was frozen, and about two feet of snow covered the ground. Kipmalook and Savokġenaq planned to be gone only for the day, so Qutuuq fixed enough food for just one meal and an afternoon snack. That day, Kipmalook would set three

traps, with Savokġenaq helping out as he began his training. Savokġenaq had the responsibility of carrying the
packsack full of food. He was dressed in fur undergarments, fur rabbit pants, fur squirrel-skin pullover,
rabbit-skin socks inside warm caribou mukluks, and a
warm outer parka with the fur toward the outside. He also
had warm wolf mittens hanging around his neck so that
when he needed to use his hands, he could just take the
mittens off without worrying that he might lose them.

Kipmalook was dressed the same. He carried the
three iron traps, the one skin for emergency bedding,
and some tough, dried moose meat. He also carried
the pouch of moose blood that he had saved so that the
animals would think that the bait was fresh meat. By
this time the blood was like a paste, so it was easy to
spread on the dried meat.

As they started to walk, Kipmalook told Savokġenaq
that they should take their time because they were
dressed so warmly. If they hurried, they would get too
hot inside all their fur clothing. He told Savokġenaq
that they had to dress warmly just in case they got stuck
somewhere. Besides, it was better to move slowly so that
they would not frighten any animals away.

When they had walked about a mile, Kipmalook
decided to set a trap where they saw wolverine tracks.

He told Savokġenaq to watch how he set it, and then he carefully put a piece of meat coated with moose blood in a spot that would not spring the trap. As he did this, he made clicking sounds so that he could keep Savokġenaq's attention. He told Savokġenaq that the spirit of an animal would be pleased to help them because they respected the animal. Then they were on their way again.

As they traveled, Kipmalook asked Savokġenaq if he was doing all right. He scouted ahead and chose where he thought it best to walk, where the snow was not deep. On this day, he was proud to have a son to teach. He wanted Savokġenaq to have a good life, and to have that, Savokġenaq needed to become a good hunter, just as Kipmalook was a good hunter.

Kipmalook found the second spot to place a trap about another mile away. They had been traveling on top of the tundra between curves in the river. Kipmalook knew that wolves and foxes roamed there because of all the tracks in the snow. He always hoped that the animals that had been caught in his traps would be dead when he got to them. It was hard for him to see the fury in their eyes from the pain of being trapped. But he knew that was his way of life and that it couldn't be changed; it was how he made a living for his family.

Kipmalook told Savokġenaq that he would be trapping for another two or three months. Then he would stop for a year because he believed that animals needed a time of peace so that they could continue to be plentiful. That lesson taught Savokġenaq not to be greedy.

About four hours had passed since they had left the sod house. They were traveling about two miles an hour, and it was near noon, because the sun was high in the sky. Even though the sun was hidden behind the clouds, Kipmalook could see where it was. They walked a while longer, until they reached a place where there were some willows. Kipmalook told Savokġenaq that they would stop there and have lunch.

Kipmalook rolled out the bear skin on the snow, and they sat down and started to chew on dried fish and some beluga muktuk and serra. After walking all that way, they both had a big appetite, and the food tasted good. Qutuuq had made a bag out of the moose stomach and filled it with tundra tea, and it was still a bit warm. They drank it right from the bag. Kipmalook told Savokġenaq not to eat too much so that he wouldn't get sleepy. They would have another snack later that day.

After they ate, cleaned up, and walked another hour, they came to the site where the whitefish was buried.

They slowly removed the stones and started digging with the siqlaq. Kipmalook decided that about five whitefish were all that he wanted to carry, so they buried the rest again and piled the same rocks on top. So far, the fish had been kept safe from any animals. Kipmalook smiled and said that Qutuuq was waiting for these aged whitefish.

Kipmalook told Savokġenaq that they would walk home on the other side of the river. They walked along the river's edge where the bushes were high and there were birch trees. When Kipmalook finally found some rabbit tracks, he set his last trap. He told Savokġenaq that he would not sell the rabbit skins; instead, Qutuuq would use them to make clothes and a blanket for the baby that would be born while they were still living up at the sod house.

This was the first time that Savokġenaq heard of a new baby. He smiled and told his papa that he hoped he would have a baby brother. Then they were on their way again. It was a little easier to walk now since there were no traps or dried meat to carry. On the way back, Kipmalook carried the packsack that Savokġenaq had been in charge of.

Back at the sod house, Qutuuq and Keenaq were busy making akutuk. Qutuuq dug out some of the dried caribou fat that she brought from home and placed about two cups of the fat in a flat wooden bowl. Then she and Keenaq chopped it together. For this, she let Keenaq use a little ulu. Qutuuq told her daughter to try to do what she was doing, and to be careful. When they were through, about half an hour later, Qutuuq started mixing the fat around and around, with one hand. Keenaq had the job of adding a few drops of water whenever Qutuuq asked her to. When the mixture turned creamy and white, Qutuuq added a little seal oil. Then she added tasty salmonberries and some blueberries to sweeten the mixture.

Qutuuq and Keenaq had fun making it together, laughing and talking, wondering how far Kipmalook and Savokġenaq were by now. Qutuuq placed the akutuk out in the entryway to keep frozen until dinner time. She knew that Kipmalook would bring some of the aged whitefish back with him. That would be dinner, along with some seal oil. Then, for dessert, they'd have the akutuk and tundra tea.

Before Kipmalook left, he had told Qutuuq that if she and Keenaq should go outside that day, not to go very far because of foxes and wolves. They knew the animals were close by because they had heard their howls the night before.

Later, when they were outside, Qutuuq made a fire at the outdoor fireplace. This helped her feel safe because she knew animals did not like fire. She put a bear skin on the ground and started to work again on softening the squirrel skins. She asked Keenaq to help her because it took so long to soften them. As they sat together, Qutuuq told her daughter the story of the blue beads, how her father and mother were so proud that they could afford to barter for them. It was a sign of wealth, meaning that her father was a great hunter and that her mother worked right along with him. Qutuuq learned how to put food away, how to help skin and dry animal furs, and how to be a wife and mother by watching her parents. She didn't know if Keenaq understood all this, but she felt like telling her anyway. She also told her daughter that they were rich now, too, because soon they would have lots of furs to barter at the trading post.

When Keenaq married, Qutuuq's earrings would be hers and Kipmalook's wedding present to her. Qutuuq said that if Keenaq's husband saw the earrings and understood what they stood for, he would want to become a great hunter himself and a good provider. Like any good mother, Qutuuq wanted her daughter to be well cared for.

When Kipmalook and Savokġenaq returned home, Qutuuq and Keenaq were still outside, and by then the tea had also been made. It was dusk, and the sky was a rosy color. The womenfolk wanted to know how they had done on their first trapping trip. The men sat down while Qutuuq served them pieces of whitefish and serra. Kipmalook told Qutuuq and Keenaq where they had set the traps and about all the animal tracks they had seen. He knew the traps were sure to catch animals; he would go and check them by himself the next day so that he could make a fast trip. Before making the two-day trapping trip, he would work on a pair of snowshoes. Then Kipmalook told Qutuuq that Savokġenaq was a strong boy, that he seemed comfortable out on the tundra, and that he did his part well and never complained. He was sure to become a great hunter someday. Qutuuq was very proud of her son.

Everyone had had a busy day, and they quickly checked the wood for the fireplace, made sure there was water, and used the outhouse. They were too tired to eat any of the akutuk. Qutuuq said that it would make a good breakfast.

While they were falling asleep, they listened to the wolves in the distance. Kipmalook knew that he would have one by the next day.

The First Catch

//////////

Kipmalook awoke early, lit the oil lamp, and talked quietly to Qutuuq. He told her to stay in bed because she needed her rest now. She smiled at him sleepily and agreed. He told her that he would be back in about five hours. He took just a little water in the waterproof bag, his little bag of dried caribou and fat, his skinning knife, and his bow and arrows, all in the skin packsack, and he was on his way.

When Kipmalook arrived at the first trap, sure enough, there was a wolverine trapped, but it was still alive. He quickly shot it with an arrow and killed it. He was glad that he did it so quickly. Sometimes trapped animals fight to stay alive. Kipmalook decided that he would skin the wolverine just in case he got something else in the other traps. When he reset the trap, he used wolverine meat for bait. He didn't need to spread any of the moose blood on it because it was fresh bait. He left the rest of the carcass on the snow, took only the skin, and set out again.

There was nothing at the second trap. The night before, as he went to sleep, he pictured a wolf at this trap. He wondered where the pack was now. Without stopping, he kept going to the third trap. There was a dead snowshoe hare in this one. It was a huge one. Kipmalook smiled because he knew Qutuuq would be happy with this rabbit. He set the trap again and headed for home. He was right; he would be home after five hours. He didn't wear as much clothing as he had on the trip with Savokġenaq, so he was able to travel faster without getting too hot in the furs.

When Kipmalook arrived home, an outdoor fire was burning again, and Savokġenaq and Keenaq were playing outside. Qutuuq was working on the squirrel skins once more and was happy to see him. Kipmalook rested and had his usual lunch, but this time with akutuk.

Later he worked on the snowshoe hare first. He was right: Qutuuq was really happy to have this rabbit. It would provide meat for their meals for the whole week—it was that large. Kipmalook told Qutuuq that this rabbit fur would be the first clothing for their new baby. She smiled at him and thanked him.

Next, there was the task of cleaning the blood off the two skins with snow. Kipmalook called the children and told them to help rub snow on them. They had fun doing this because it ended in a snow fight. Even Kipmalook was on the ground tickling Qutuuq. He loved to listen to her laugh because, when she laughed, it made everyone laugh. After that, they all sat and took a break.

Tomorrow would be time enough to cut tiny holes all around the furs so that they could be stretched on the willow racks he had made. Kipmalook felt that everything was going as planned, that a Great Maker was watching over them and that his little family was happy and safe.

The next day, they all were busy as usual. Qutuuq told Kipmalook that before he went on his two-day trapping trip, they had to make sure every detail was taken care of. After they had eaten breakfast and were drinking their tea, they started to plan. Today they would stretch the skins. Then Kipmalook would take the children and look for the right willow to make his snowshoes, while Qutuuq stayed at home and worked on the skins.

Qutuuq wanted to sit inside the sod house while working on the rabbit so that her hands wouldn't get so cold. As she worked, she talked to the spirit of the rabbit, thanking it for letting them have it. She decided that she would cook the legs and cut some of the other meat into squares so that she could cook them on a stick by the fireplace. Then she made a second batch ready to boil for the next day. There was still a lot of meat, so she prepared the rest to have for two more meals and took those out to the food cache. It was below freezing now, so the meat could be preserved for later use.

As she watched the meat to make sure it didn't burn, Qutuuq thought about Kipmalook's shaman parents and their beliefs. They had given her a charm: a dried stomach of a tiny smelt fish. They didn't want her to have a big stomach for some reason. When she was around them, she gave them respect, but she didn't really believe what they believed. She felt her stomach and thought to herself, "I won't have a small stomach for long."

Qutuuq was glad that they were not living in the same village as Kipmalook's parents. Every time Savokġenaq spent time with them, she was worried. Savokġenaq knew how to express himself well and would report to his parents what his grandparents did. Every time, Kalineq would do a ritual: he would pack Savokġenaq on his back to try to pass the shaman power to him.

Once, Savokġenaq told Qutuuq and Kipmalook, "In the shaman's house there is a small platform. Grandpa took off his parka and was bare-chested. He showed his audience a little jagged piece of willow with branches on it. When he started his performance, both Grandpa and Grandma chanted a song. Then I saw him stick the willow into his stomach on the left side under the ribs. I saw blood on the willow branches, but there was no hole. He stuck it in the left side and it came out on the right side. Then he pushed it back in the right side and it came out on the left side. Still there were no holes or blood on him when he showed his audience."

Qutuuq thought that once in a while, shamans felt they had to show the villagers that they had powers and that this helped them keep their status. She knew that what Savokġenaq had told them was what he thought he had seen, but for her, there was a greater power. She didn't know what it was yet, but she knew that there was a Great Maker because all life seemed to unfold in an orderly manner.

Just then a piece of the meat sizzled, and Qutuuq got busy and stopped thinking about her in-laws. Everywhere around the little sod house smelled so good with the barbecuing meat. When the rabbit was done, she was happy that dinner was ready for later.

Qutuuq thought she had better get started sewing the undergarments for everyone. The oil lamp was lit, so there would be more light to see where to stitch. She was an expert seamstress and knew exactly where to start. First, she would make a new garment for Kipmalook. If she worked steadily on it, she could be through in about a week. She told herself that this is what she would do whenever she wasn't helping Kipmalook with the furs.

Several hours later, her family came home, and all were hungry. She fed them the usual lunch and told them that the delicious meat was for dinner. When they came in, Kipmalook said that it was getting stormy outside. They all had carried big bundles of willow and were tired. Since it was getting stormy, they thought it would be a good idea to take a short nap.

Keenaq started to fuss a little. Whenever she did that, Qutuuq would sing her a little song:

Kiggitat akulliatni,
Chungelaqmik Koweyaq tal lig mik,
Mamchunquk tal lig mik,
Iigit ta ha, iigit ta ha,

Ha ya i cha ma,
Ha ya ya i yach cha ma,
There is an island between.
In place of sand,
It is full of mud and driftwood.
Let's get in, let's get in.
Ha ya i cha ma,
Ha ya ya i yach cha ma.

When she finished, Keenaq had stopped fussing and everyone went to lie down. Qutuuq believed in disciplining her children the same way her mother had disciplined her. Most parents knew to distract little children who were fussing by singing or trying to make them join in with laughter. When children got a bit older, like Savokġenaq, adults spent a lot of time with them, letting them observe how things were done and talking to them about what was right and what was wrong. When boys became teenagers, an uncle or another member of the village would help in teaching them how to hunt. But this winter, Kipmalook would be Savokġenaq's teacher; that had been the purpose of the one-day trapline trip.

When Qutuuq and Kipmalook awoke, it was late afternoon. Savokġenaq got up for a while, too, and stoked the fire by putting more willows on the coals. They were burning alder willow, which burned a long time, leaving good coals. After stoking the fire, Savokġenaq went back inside and fell asleep again. He had become a big help on this journey.

Illness Appears

//////////

This nap was the first one the family had taken since coming upriver in early Fall. They had been too busy getting settled in for the winter to rest much. Qutuuq was glad that Kipmalook had napped so that he would not be so tired when he started out on his two-day trapline. Kipmalook said he would make his snowshoes the next day and leave the day after.

As Kipmalook lay there talking to Qutuuq, he noticed, for the first time, a lump on his neck near his throat. He asked her to feel it. They both wondered what it could be.

Qutuuq asked him, "How do you feel?"

He answered that he didn't feel any different. "Maybe it will go away just like it appeared," he told her.

Then they started to talk about their little family. Keenaq and Savokġenaq were never sick, except for the times when their baby teeth were coming in. At those times, when they felt a bit feverish and fussy, Qutuuq peeled the little willows they used for fever. One would be wound like a teething ring, and the baby would be made to chew on it. That would always help, and there was never any great concern because the parents knew that this discomfort was a natural part of growing up. Qutuuq was never sick either, except for being uncomfortable during her menstrual cycle.

When she mentioned this, Kipmalook chuckled and said, "I'm glad I wasn't born a woman!"

"You would have been an ugly woman anyway!" she told him. And they both started to laugh.

Kipmalook got up first. He went outside to check the weather. When he came back in he said that it was really stormy, so he had stoked the fire and arranged the hot stones on it. He told Qutuuq to stay in bed, that he would make the tea. Both Savokġenaq and Keenaq were still asleep.

As Kipmalook sat waiting for the stones to heat up, he thought about the lump he had found. He really was a bit worried, but he did not want to show his worry to Qutuuq. He told himself that he would put every minute into the business of trapping and working on the furs. He would go out for two days and then work on the skins the following day.

That night as they sat in their little sod house listening to the storm outside, Kipmalook started to play the drum. At first, he just drummed, and no one sang. It was like an introduction. Then they sang all the songs and dances that they already knew. Savokġenaq danced the seal-hunt dance; Keenaq a berry-picking dance. Then Qutuuq did the crane dance. When she was through, she asked Kipmalook to give the drum to her. As she started to drum and sing, she chose the polar-bear dance. She loved to watch Kipmalook do that dance, which he had learned from his friends on one of his trips north. It expressed a message of courage and great strength. Those were the qualities she saw in her husband.

The next day, while the children played out in the fresh snow making a village scene, Kipmalook and Qutuuq started to work on their projects inside the sod house. It was now too cold to work outside with bare hands. Qutuuq sat close by the oil lamp so she could keep it going while working on Kipmalook's new undergarment. Kipmalook got busy making himself crude snowshoes out of willow and rawhide. As they worked, they exchanged stories about their families.

While they were talking, the children ran in to warm up.

"Listen while I tell you a story," Qutuuq said to them.

"Once there lived a grandma and an orphan boy. The boy told his grandma that he wanted to go beach-combing. His grandma told him that would be okay, that he might find something to eat. First, he found a tomcod fish. He cut off the head and ate it whole. He was still hungry, so when he found a seal, he did the same thing. He was still hungry, and when he found a white whale, he did the same thing. He cut off the head and ate it whole. Then he was thirsty. He found a freshwater pond and drank the whole pond. Afterward, he was still thirsty and found another pond and drank almost that whole pond. Now, he was finally satisfied.

"He started walking home very slowly because he was so full. When he got to the door, he couldn't fit through. He tried to go into a hole in the roof that was also used as a smoke vent. When he still couldn't get in, he asked his poor grandma, singing a little tune that went, 'Where could I go in?' Finally his grandma answered back with a tune, saying, 'Through this poor little door, come in.' The orphan boy sang back to her, 'I'm too big. I'll get stuck. I can't go through the door.' To which the grandma sang back to him, 'Through my needle hole, come in!'

"In a split second, he was in. By this time, he was also cold and started to warm up by the fire. After standing there for a while, his belly broke, flooding the room. The grandma got into a wooden container, grabbed a wooden spoon, and paddled out the door.

"As she was paddling, the grandma said, 'When you get so very hungry, you have to remember to eat just a little bit.'"

Qutuuq said, "*A, koe, mae!*" declaring it the end of the story. Then she asked her children, "Are you hungry yet?"

"No!" they both yelled and ran back outside to play. Kipmalook and Qutuuq laughed and then worked quietly for a long time. They both wanted to finish what they were doing. He was intertwining the rawhide on his snowshoes, and she was just about through sewing the part that fit on the front and back of Kipmalook's top undergarment.

At one point while working on her sewing, Qutuuq went outdoors quickly to make tea. They stopped only briefly to eat crackers, dried fish, and serra. By the time they finished working that night, Kipmalook was through with his snowshoes, and Qutuuq had just a little bit of trim to sew around the neck and the wrists of Kipmalook's undergarment. She would use a strip of rabbit in both places. She told herself that while Kipmalook was up on the trapline, she would begin sewing an undergarment for herself. It's always good to have an extra one.

Kipmalook Begins the Two-Day Trip

//////////

The next morning, when Kipmalook got up, he went outside to stretch and check the weather. He stood in one place for a minute and looked in the direction that he would be heading. The sky was overcast, but he knew it wasn't going to storm anymore, at least not in the next two days that he would be working on his trapline. He stayed outside and started the fire, putting on the heating rocks. It was about six o'clock—he wanted to get an early start.

Soon Qutuuq got up. She knew she had to pack the food for Kipmalook's trip. They both knew what to do and went about working while the children slept. Qutuuq cut up the dried moose meat and made sure there was enough for six meals. Then she went outside to the food cache and got some of the serra that had moose liver and heart preserved in it. She knew that would taste good when Kipmalook ate outside and had only the dried meat. She also got out a piece of white muktuk to cut into bite-size pieces. She put all the serra and white muktuk together in a bag made of ugruk intestines. The dried meat she placed inside the packsack. Then she filled the moose-stomach bag half full of water out of the birch basket where they kept the water for daily use. As she poured some water into the bag, she reminded her husband to put bottom-snow in it every once in a while so that he would have water all the time.

Then Qutuuq checked Kipmalook's clothing. The river was frozen, so he would wear his winter muk-luks. Inside of those, he had rabbit-fur socks. He had on both his undergarments made out of squirrel skin. They were worn, but they were more comfortable that way. Next came outer pants made of moose hide and a parka made out of caribou. On the ruff was wolver-ine, and wolf-skin mitts would hang on a string around Kipmalook's neck. Qutuuq checked the clothing for any rips that she should repair. When there weren't any, she was relieved. She was proud of herself because she always tried to keep her family well clothed by sewing constantly.

Kipmalook checked his snowshoes once more and then checked his bow and arrows. He made sure that he had his arrows for a wolf and a wolverine.

He thought to himself, "Those two animals sure think they're better than each other." He smiled because they were right. "Each is better than the other in certain ways. So don't forget to use the right arrows when you have to."

He had an arrow for a fox. A fox—whether it was a blue fox or red fox—was a class below the wolf and wolverine. He was sure a wolf or wolverine spirit would be insulted if he used an arrow on it that was made for a fox. If he trapped a lynx, he could use a wolf arrow because a lynx was just as fierce as a wolf and their spirits had respect for each other. He also took arrows for a ptarmigan and a rabbit.

When Kipmalook was ready to leave, they sat down for a breakfast of crackers, tea, and akutuk, which Qutuuq always had on hand in the entryway. They kept their voices low.

"Make sure that the children don't play on the river," said Kipmalook.

Sometimes, even at this time of the year, there could be some overflow. He didn't want to worry about the children while he was away. His wife assured him that she would watch after them. Then he told her not to work too hard because when he returned with the furs, she would be working hard again. Qutuuq told him that she would just take care of the children and sew the squirrel-skin undergarments. She hoped to finish the little that was left on his and then start on hers while he was gone.

"When I make mine, it will have to be wider in the middle," she said.

It made them both think of the baby that would be born in the spring. They smiled at each other.

Kipmalook crawled over to kiss each of his sleeping children on the forehead, and then he and his wife kissed on the lips, making a little sound. Qutuuq followed him outside.

She watched him fix his packsack. First, he attached the little bear skin that he would be sleeping on. The head and legs and arms were cut off so it was just light enough to pack. Then came the snowshoes, placed close to his back. On top of those were the grub bag and the gun and ammunition. Then the bow was attached so that he could get at it in an emergency if he had to. He also kept the arrows right by the bow, easy to reach. When he started to walk, they smiled at each other once more. There was no good-bye, maybe because they knew that they would always be thinking of each other.

Qutuuq watched Kipmalook walk on the riverbank. The river seemed frozen, but because he had told her not to let the children on the ice, she knew that he would walk on land as much as possible. She watched until he was out of sight. Then she stooped over and went back through the entryway.

Kipmalook walked slowly. He always did walk as if he were sneaking up on something. He walked slowly because he was dressed so warmly and did not want to sweat. It was not long before he came to deep snow, so he stopped and put on his snowshoes. Walking was then much easier. As he walked, he heard only the sound of the snowshoes hitting the day-old snow. He followed the curve of the river, stopping only to look around. The ground was very white, so he put on his sunglasses made from ivory with narrow slits for viewing. As he walked, he listened for the sounds of animals, but he heard only a weak wind. He liked that wind, for it was just enough to keep him from getting too warm. On most of the trail, the tall willows were a little farther back from the river's edge, making it easy to walk. Back behind the willows, there were tall white birch trees. Beyond the trees were the mountains.

By that time, Kipmalook had reached the hill on which Qutuuq had picked cranberries. When he was up on that hill last fall, he had planned this trapline. Now he would travel all along the bank of the river until he reached a mountain about eight to ten miles away. He knew it would take him all day to reach the mountain and set traps along the way. Sometimes he walked a few yards back into the willows to set a trap; then the next time he set a trap a few feet back from the river. Each time, he smeared some of the old moose blood on the bait.

After Kipmalook had set four traps, which was about six hours later, he stopped and had his lunch of dried moose meat and serra. To keep up his strength, he knew that he must have some seal oil every time that he ate. While he was eating, he wondered how his family was doing. He was thankful that his wife was self-sufficient. He knew she took pride in being able to help him with all the animal furs that he brought home. Qutuuq knew that those blue beads her parents had given her were a symbol of status in the village and that being able to work with the skins and sew all the clothes for the family were all a part of that status. Kipmalook also knew she was proud of him, and that made him feel good. With that thought, he told himself that he better get going.

Before finishing for the day, he had two more traps to set, and he wanted to walk back toward the mountains to set them. It was hard walking through the willows because of deep snow, but walking through the birch trees was very beautiful. Among the trees, he noticed lots of rabbit tracks. He told himself to pass those tracks because he would rather catch big game on this trapline. He walked in toward the mountains and up for about two hours. Nearing the end of the birch trees, he could plainly see the mountain where he wanted to set the traps. The last trap was set on a little slope right under the mountain.

With all the traps set, Kipmalook looked around for the best place to camp for the night. He found one near a huge birch tree. For some reason, he always chose something that he felt might protect him. He could either go behind the tree or try to climb it if he had to. He took off his packsack but wouldn't open his fur mattress until it was time to use it, just in case he had to leave in a hurry. He decided that he would gather some dead branches, enough wood to keep a fire burning the whole night. Wild animals did not like fire.

Then, because it was still early, Kipmalook scouted around his camp to hunt ptarmigan at the same time. He didn't have to go far before he spotted a flock under some short bushes. He moved very slowly and quietly. As Kipmalook looked at the ptarmigan, it seemed as if they didn't know he was there. He shot one, and the rest flew away. He knew that ptarmigan didn't fly very far. He followed them four more times and killed two more. He reminded himself that he would have to carry furs back, so maybe three ptarmigan were enough. Kipmalook was happy. He was finally starting to feel tired from all the walking and trapping he had done that day, so he started back toward camp.

Remembering
Savokgenaq's Birth

/////////

Back at home, Qutuuq did the usual chores, and so did her children. Afterward, Savokġenaq and Keenaq played outside while Qutuuq stayed in and finished Kipmalook's undergarment. She reminded both of the children two or three times not to go on the river because their papa told them not to.

Soon Qutuuq started on her own undergarment. This was her third baby. As she sewed her maternity undergarment, she thought back to the time when she gave birth to Savokġenaq, her firstborn.

It was in the fall and not too cold yet. Her family had been at the mouth of the next river up from where they lived. They had been there picking berries after putting away dried fish and hunting ducks. Her mother, Icharaq, took her to a spot on the top of a little hill. She told her that when the time came, she should come up here by herself and give birth. No one was allowed to be with her, not even another woman. Qutuuq remembered how frightened she was at the thought of doing that. Her mother told her if she didn't do that, it would bring bad luck to the men who were hunting—that the men believe they cannot be near a woman giving birth. If they couldn't hunt successfully anymore, the whole community would know whose fault it was. Then she and her family would be shunned.

When the time came, Qutuuq was in so much pain every time she had a contraction that she didn't mind being alone up on the hill. She remembered lying on top of the hill hollering every time she had a pain. It took a whole day of labor for Savokġenaq to be born.

Finally, when Savokġenaq was born, she grabbed him and cut off the umbilical cord and put him in a skin that she had brought with her. Savokġenaq cried right away. He probably felt the brisk fall air. Quickly, she checked his whole body while wrapping him up. Her mother had explained what to do. Although she would be uncomfortable, her mother had told her to keep pushing for a few minutes after the baby was born. When she did that, the afterbirth came, and to her that was painful. After, she sat for a long time.

"That wasn't that hard," she thought to herself.

Qutuuq cleaned the baby with the tundra moss that grew everywhere around her. She noticed that he just wanted to sleep. She talked to him and told him to sleep all he wanted. When she got back to the camp, she would sleep also. Some time passed. Then, after taking care of the baby and burying the afterbirth with tundra moss, Qutuuq walked back to their camp. That day she was happy to hand her baby over to her mother so that she could rest.

That was nine years ago. Two years later, Keenaq was born. Having Keenaq was easier because Qutuuq was experienced, having had one baby. Keenaq was born near a village in the north when she and Kipmalook, along with her parents, were coming back from a bartering trip. Those trips north were always exciting, and Qutuuq wasn't about to stay home just because she was going to have a baby. They enjoyed making new friends and seeing friends they had made before. So, along the way, when Qutuuq was starting to go into labor, Kipmalook, who was captain of the boat, went to shore with his wife and told her to go up on land until they couldn't hear her screaming. And that's what she did. This birth took only four hours. Qutuuq was glad for that.

When she came back to the boat, Qutuuq was given some food and something to drink. Icharaq took the baby from her while she rested for a couple of hours. Later, while they were sitting around the campfire, her mother gave the baby a name, Keenaq, after a relative who had died. In their family, newborn babies were given the names of people whose characteristics the family admired. A male baby might be given the name of someone who was a great hunter or who was known for being a kind person. A female baby might be given the name of a person who was a good storyteller or a fast runner. When babies were given the names of adult-deceased people, the family believed they shouldn't be disciplined for fear that the spirit might get angry and leave the baby's body. If the spirit left the body, it was believed that the child might become crippled or die.

Just then, Qutuuq became startled. It was so quiet that she thought she better stop sewing and go check on her children. They were dressed warmly and never got cold, so they played outside long hours. Even when they came in sometimes and said they were cold, Qutuuq knew they were coming in just because they were curious about what was going on inside the sod house. She put on her parka, in case they weren't right outside, and went out. When she found them, they were busy making a snow house a few yards away. When they saw their mother coming, they both gave her a big smile. Qutuuq told them that she was just checking on them and that they should come inside in a while to eat and do the evening chores. Before she went back in, she put wood on the fire along with the rocks to make tea for supper. Then, in the sod house, she fixed the oil lamp and continued to sew her maternity garment.

On the Long Trapline

Up the river, Kipmalook gathered more wood to make sure he didn't run out during the night. When he camped out like this, he woke every couple of hours. Just before it started to get dark, he took his ivory blade and gutted the three ptarmigan. He didn't feel like cooking any right then. Qutuuq had already made sure that all his meals were taken care of, so he sat down and ate some of the packed food and planned when he would come back this way to check the trapline.

He would go home tomorrow, and they would stretch the skins the next day. The day after that, he would take Savokġenaq on the short trapline and stretch those skins the very same day. Then he would go out on the long trapline again. In all, Kipmalook wanted to make eight trips on the long trapline, and with six traps, he probably would trap four animals each time. That would be about thirty-two skins plus perhaps two skins from every trip on the short trapline, making about forty skins in all. If he didn't reach forty, then he would plan to go out a couple more times. As he ate some serra, he was happy to find that Qutuuq had mixed in some of the cooked, aged liver and heart. That sure tasted good out here with the dried moose and pieces of white muktuk. Then, thinking of Qutuuq, he remembered that she had said to put more bottom-snow in his water pouch. So he did that after he finished his dinner.

When Kipmalook was ready for bed, he fixed the fire and lay down on his fur mattress, using his packsack for a pillow. He was so tired that it didn't take him long to fall asleep. Every time he woke up during the night, he automatically put wood on the fire. It wasn't like sleeping at home in the sod house, where he felt safe. It was when he awoke the third time that he heard wolves howling. The sounds were coming from the direction of the traps up on the hill. He curled into a ball and went back to sleep, knowing he should be safe by the fire with his bow and arrows right by his hand.

Kipmalook woke up earlier than he normally did at home. He got up, anxious to get started even before he ate anything. He would check the two traps on the hill and then return to the fire to eat before heading back along the trapline toward home. That morning he felt stiff from sleeping curled up to stay warm, but he knew he'd feel more limber by the time he got back to the fire.

"No snowshoes for this part of the trapline," he said to himself.

The only things Kipmalook took were his bow and arrows. If he got two animals, he would drag them back to this camp to skin. As he started to walk, he realized that he should have worn his snowshoes because he was sinking with every footstep.

"Keep going," he told himself; yet he couldn't believe that he had made the wrong decision already this morning.

Although Kipmalook thought of himself as young and strong, he was huffing and puffing by the time he arrived at the first trap. What greeted him there was a wolf that looked exhausted and frightened. Every time Kipmalook found a trapped animal that was still alive, he had to put aside his feelings and try to think about feeding his family. This one wolf skin would be worth some of those crackers that his family loved to eat. How he wished that this animal were already dead.

When he killed the wolf, he spoke to it, saying, "There, you can rest."

Then Kipmalook reset the trap and headed toward the second one, dragging the dead wolf. When he reached the trap he was happy to find that the wolf in it was dead. He thought to himself that this probably was a weak animal.

After resetting the trap, Kipmalook looked toward his camp and thought he saw a shorter way to get there. As he started walking down the hill, he tripped on the little ridge of his footprint. He hollered to himself to "Hang on!" He hung on to the two wolves that he was dragging, fell face forward, and the hill took him down toward his camp. The fur on his parka was in the right direction, making it slick on the snow. After sliding all the way down to the bottom of the little hill, he just lay there and laughed until he felt weak. When he finally stopped laughing, he thought to himself, "What a story I'll have to tell Qutuuq when I get home."

When he stood up and looked around, he really was closer to his camp than if he had gone back the way he had come. He rearranged his grip on the two wolf carcasses and headed off toward his camp. When he got there he realized that his body wasn't stiff anymore and that he was now thinking more clearly. He put more wood on the coals that he had kept burning all night. That morning, his breakfast of dried moose, muktuk, and serra tasted especially good. He had worked up a big appetite.

Kipmalook skinned the two wolves very quickly. He told himself that if everything went well that day, he could be home in time for dinner with his family. This time he put on his snowshoes and then slowly started to walk back along his trapline. Along the way, he smiled to himself whenever he thought about what had happened back on the little hill.

A while later, as Kipmalook was walking, his parka hood got caught on a willow. Instead of taking the time to put down the two furs, he tried to pull his hood loose by walking and tugging. The willow was too thick to pull free from, and it pulled him back after he took two steps. Still holding the two wet skins, he sat down on the ground and couldn't believe that something foolish had happened to him again. This time he didn't laugh right away. He was starting to get tired again.

Kipmalook decided it might be wise to rest for a while, so he sat down on his skin and thought about his trapping plans. What an uncle had told him was really true. "When you have respect for all of life, the animals will know that," his uncle had said. Kipmalook would stick to his plan of making at least eight trips on his trapline and then stopping and giving the animals a rest. As he sat there, he wondered what it was like where these traps—which he'd bartered for at his village's trading post—came from. Someday, he would like to find out.

He was also thinking about what the Russians looked like. The man who ran the trading post was half Russian and had light skin and light hair, and he wondered about the Russian people. What was it like where they came from? The people also told stories about how the Russians traveled by ship; that was how they brought supplies to their trading posts. It was getting close to noon. Kipmalook could tell by the sun. He definitely had time to rest a little longer, and he decided to take a nap. Since it was daytime, he felt he didn't need a fire to be safe.

Kipmalook napped easily. He was awakened a short time later when a cold wind hit his face. He jumped up and quickly packed the skins. Right now he would be happy if there were no other animals in the three remaining traps because he wanted to start walking home to the sod house.

There were no animals in the next two traps. The last one, near the riverbank, held a snowshoe hare. Now Kipmalook could head home. As he was walking along, the sun shone for a while. When he put on his sunglasses, he was suddenly anxious to make a trip north again to see his friends and trade for more ivory. Maybe next summer his family and Qutuuq's parents could go again. Perhaps they could make one more trip together before his in-laws got too old to travel that far. He would discuss the idea with Qutuuq while they worked on the skins the next two days.

A Successful Six Weeks

//////////

While Kipmalook was making his way back home, everything was running smoothly at the little sod house. Qutuuq was working hard to finish sewing new undergarments for herself and Kipmalook. His was done, and now she was now working on the sleeves of hers. She told herself that she would start on the children's the next time Kipmalook was gone on the trapline.

Savokġenaq and Keenaq were playing out in front of the sod house as their father came around the last bend. When they saw him, they both yelled, "Papa's home!" and ran toward him. When they reached him, he stopped and smiled at both of them and touched them on the head. Savokġenaq took his pack and Keenaq took his snowshoes.

Qutuuq had been expecting her husband around this time, so she had hot tea ready and was heating water to cook whatever he was bringing home. She quickly slipped on her mukluks before going outside. She and Kipmalook were happy to see each other and told each other so. Before they went inside, they brought the skins Kipmalook had brought back to the food cache. They would wait until the next day to stretch them. Right now they would just skin the rabbit and then sit down for dinner. Qutuuq always did this task inside at her work area.

While she was working on the rabbit, Kipmalook sat and drank some tea. He started to tell them his story about sliding down the hill early that morning. He told them how when he got up, he was tired and stiff and apparently wasn't thinking straight when he left his snowshoes at the camp. Then he described how he tripped and fell headfirst and kept sliding on his fur parka down the hill, and how, when he got to the bottom, he was still holding on to both of the wolf skins. His story made everyone laugh because they had never seen their papa slide down any hill before. Then he told them how he couldn't stop laughing when he had finally stopped at the bottom of the hill. Kipmalook looked at his children and said, "I might go sliding with you someday." The children looked at each other and grinned from ear to ear.

The next day, they all were busy working on the skins. When Kipmalook and Qutuuq worked together, they worked fast. They stretched the skins and tied them down on top of the drying rack they had made for drying moose meat. It was surely the beginning of a successful fur-trapping season. When they were through that day, they both stood back and admired the three skins that were stretched.

That night, after another dinner of fresh rabbit meat and akutuk, they decided to celebrate, and Qutuuq had her ceremony giving thanks. Everyone did their favorite dances, and then they did the new song and dance they would be performing back in the village.

Before going to sleep that night, Kipmalook asked Qutuuq how she felt with the new baby coming. She told him that when he was gone she was remembering how she had given birth to the other children. Although he didn't ask, she reassured him that she would be fine again when she gave birth to this baby.

The next day, after the morning chores were done, Kipmalook and Savokġenaq went off on the one-day trapline again. Kipmalook told his son to use the snowshoes and that he would trail behind him without snowshoes. Then he laughed and said there was no hill to slide down on. Before they left, Qutuuq asked them to bring back some whitefish from the place where it was buried. They told her that they would and went on their way. As they were walking, Kipmalook told his son to take his time, that you never knew when you might run into an animal and you wanted to have time to get the bow and arrow ready. They walked along slowly and quietly, and Kipmalook noticed how strong and coordinated Savokġenaq was. He knew that Savokġenaq, too, would become a great hunter.

At every one of the four traps, foxes had been caught. There was one blue fox and three red ones. They skinned two of the animals and then each dragged one home, stopping to retrieve some of the whitefish Qutuuq wanted.

Qutuuq was glad to see all four foxes when they brought them home. That evening was spent skinning the two remaining foxes by the fire outside. Somehow, when one was happy, it didn't feel cold working outside. At the end of that day, they had seven skins drying.

The next six weeks went pretty much according to plan. Kipmalook trapped at least four animals on the long trapline and maybe two on the short trapline every time out. The family was very busy. All of them were so used to the schedule that the days seemed to fly by, and none of them got tired of the work or the routine. The skins were starting to pile up in the food cache, and they wanted to see if the pile would go clear to the top. Although Qutuuq was tired every night, she forced herself to do some sewing on the children's undergarments before she went to bed. Eventually, those were finished too. She decided that her next project would be making mukluks for Savokġenaq and Keenaq.

Once in a while, Kipmalook would let Qutuuq feel the size of the lump that was growing on his neck. It wasn't going away. He kept telling himself that maybe it would disappear, but instead, he found himself feeling sick while out checking his traps one day. As he walked along his trapline, Kipmalook felt nauseous, and that night, as he lay on his skin mattress, his body was covered with sweat. He was too sick to climb the hill to check the farthest two traps. He told himself that he would just walk home the next day without checking any more traps because he couldn't work on the skins. He would make another trip when he felt better. When he tried to eat, he couldn't. He did drink some water, but not very much.

As Kipmalook slowly made his way back home the following day, he wondered to himself if the spirits were angry with him for trapping too many animals. Maybe he had become too greedy. He would go home and ask Qutuuq to help make him well and to ask the spirits of the animals to forgive him for wanting too many furs.

Taking Care of Kipmalook

※※※※※

That morning Qutuuq had felt uneasy about something, but she didn't know what. She decided it would be a good day to sleep in because once Kipmalook got home, they would be busy working on the skins for the next two days. The children were still asleep, so she told herself not to worry. Her uneasiness was probably from being pregnant.

When Qutuuq went back to sleep, the dreams came. She could see Kipmalook standing on an ice floe, unable to jump ashore. As she yelled at him to jump, the current moved the ice farther away. When she started to cry in her dream, she suddenly awoke and realized she had been dreaming; so she turned over and went back to sleep again. In her next dream, she and her two children were standing on a riverbank during break-up. That day, Kipmalook had gone out to hunt for muskrats. As they stood there, the ice started to move swiftly. Suddenly,

Kipmalook was being swept away on the ice in the middle of the river. There was nothing anyone could do. This time, all three of them were crying. When Qutuuq awoke from this dream, she sat up and wiped her eyes, disbelieving that it was only a dream.

Now she got up from her fur mattress on the floor. The children were still sleeping, and she was glad that they were. She felt very tired from having had bad dreams. As she lifted the bear skin to go outside, she looked at the sky. It was a dull gray. To her that meant that it would snow that day.

As Qutuuq stood there, she realized that the riverbank a few yards away was where they were standing in the dream watching Kipmalook being swept away. While walking toward the outhouse, the uneasy feeling came back. "It was nothing but a dream," she tried to reassure herself.

On her way back to the sod house, Qutuuq went to the food cache. She saw they had a lot of skins. She knew that she should feel happy to see so much fur, but for some reason, she wasn't that happy. Instead, she reached over for some of the dried moose meat, taking inventory of how much was left. There wasn't much.

"Maybe Kipmalook will bring home a rabbit today so that we can have some fresh meat," she said to herself.

When Qutuuq returned to the sod house and was straightening the wick on the oil lamp, she felt the baby move for the first time. She held her hand on her stomach and started to hum and then sing quietly to the baby.

Iglu keta, mina oo ma mi yu ma,
Akule qut ta mina oo ma mi yu ma,
Inqiq tal lig mik,
Kilqiq tal lig mik,
Kiggitat akulliatni,
Chungelaqmik, koweyaq tal lig mik,
Mamchunquk tal lig mik,
Iigit ta ha, iigit ta ha,
Ha ya I cha ma,
Ha ya ya I yach cha ma,

If I were a seagull, I would be throwing rocks,
If I were a seagull in a place called Aakule qut ta,
Where there is a mountain,
Where there is a ptarmigan hawk,
There is an island between,
In place of sand, there is mud and driftwood
It's a steep riverbank,
Let's get in, let's get in.

Ha ya i cha ma,
Ha ya ya I yach cha ma.

When Qutuuq finished singing, she remembered that it was her mother who had taught her this song. It was in a dialect from south of their village. Especially in the summer time, at a place with lots of rocks on the beach, her mother would juggle two smooth little rocks and sing this song at the same time. Sometimes she would juggle two or three times through. Qutuuq realized that her mother was using this song to entertain her. She told herself that she would try to do more fun things with her own children. In her heart, she thanked her mother for teaching her, though at the time she hadn't realized that she was being taught.

That morning, after breakfast, all three worked together cleaning out their little dwelling.

"Take one fur each outside and pound on it with a stick," Qutuuq said to Savokġenaq and Keenaq. As they pounded on the furs, she kept time to the song that she was singing earlier.

"Sing with me," she said to her children. They sang and pounded until all the furs were clean. Then they continued to sing and started to dance until all three of them ended up on the ground laughing.

Qutuuq noticed that Keenaq was looking up the river into the distance. She followed with her eyes and realized that it was Kipmalook. They watched for a full minute and were surprised to see that it was really him. They weren't expecting him until the evening because it usually took him two full days to work his trapline.

"Something must be wrong," Qutuuq said.

They all ran to meet Kipmalook. They were so surprised that they ran on the frozen river, even though Kipmalook had told them to stay off the river in case it might be dangerous. When he saw them coming, he, too, started walking on the river. That walk seemed like a lifetime for both Qutuuq and Kipmalook. Each knew that something was not right.

When the family finally reached him, Savokġenaq grabbed his father's packsack, and Qutuuq handed the snowshoes to Keenaq. Without talking, everyone knew what to do. Qutuuq felt the fever but wondered if Kipmalook was so hot because he had been hurrying to reach home. After they had walked a few yards, with Qutuuq's hands around Kipmalook's waist trying to keep him up, she finally asked him, "What happened out there? Why are you so sick?"

Kipmalook struggled to answer her. "Last night, the fever came, and I couldn't check any traps."

Then she said, "Don't worry now. I will take you home and put you to bed."

Qutuuq noticed that her husband seemed to be out of breath. She stopped and told him to sit down for a while. He couldn't sit down, so she helped him lie down and gently rest his head on the frozen river. Qutuuq sat very close to him and told the children to sit down too. They were both frightened and puzzled because usually when their Papa came home, he was happy and talking about his trip.

They sat there quietly for about an hour while Kipmalook slept. Eventually Keenaq slept by her papa, too. Savokġenaq was old enough to know that something was very wrong just by the look on his mother's face, and he couldn't sleep.

Qutuuq reached inside the hood on Kipmalook's parka. As she did that, she was hoping that she wouldn't feel the growth on his neck. To her dismay, the growth seemed larger than the last time they had talked about it.

Savokġenaq asked his mother, "Is that why Papa is sick?"

She nodded her head slowly and said, "It is why Papa is sick. But when we get home, I will make some stinkweed broth and let him drink it. Then I will make some paste from it and put some on his neck."

Qutuuq tried to sound reassuring, but she knew they had never dealt with anything like this before. The broth always helped and was used when they became too exhausted from working so hard, and the paste helped when someone got a cut. Savokġenaq nodded his head and held on to his mother's arm. He closed his eyes and lay there.

While Kipmalook slept on the frozen river, Qutuuq sat and watched all three of them. If they were out there at any other time, she would have been watching for wild animals. This time she was so worried about her husband being sick that she was not afraid of animals. In her mind, she was trying to will his sickness away and give him some of the strength from her own body. She remembered the willows she had put away for helping with fever. After Kipmalook woke up, she would take him home, put him to bed, and then prepare a fever medicine from the willow bark. Remembering this, she felt some relief and was sure that, with good care, she would make him well.

When Kipmalook finally woke up, he seemed to be more aware than when they had found him. Qutuuq shook little Keenaq and told her to get up because they were going home now. It took them some time to reach the sod house, which was only a short distance away and should have taken just a while if everything were normal. As Qutuuq walked slowly, with her arm around her husband's waist, she gave him lots of encouragement. She kept telling him that he would feel better after she gave him medicine; that in a few days he would be up and about and checking his traplines again; that he did the right thing by just coming home; and that he shouldn't worry about anything.

Qutuuq asked Savokġenaq to check the fire and to put on more wood to heat the cooking rocks to make hot water. She laid Kipmalook down on the clean bed in the sod house and told him to rest. As she was taking off his outer garments, she felt how hot and damp they were. She decided to take off his inner garment so that he could cool down and dry off.

Once he was lying down comfortably, Qutuuq said to her children, "Come with me. Let's go and get the medicine from the cache. Savokġenaq, you'll have to climb up and hand it down to me. And Keenaq, you can help carry it back."

As they were walking back from the cache, Keenaq asked her mother, "Will Papa get better?"

Qutuuq told her not to worry, that all three of them would help make him well. "See, we're starting already. With your help, Papa can only get better."

With that comment, Keenaq smiled and felt better and not so afraid.

In a wooden bowl, Qutuuq crushed some dry stinkweed leaves with a little stone. Before that, she had lit the seal-oil lamp so there would be light to work by, telling herself all the while that she shouldn't use too much seal oil because their supply was getting low. In the flickering light of the oil lamp, all three sat on the floor listening to the sound of the stone grinding on the wooden bowl. When Qutuuq had ground a little less than a cup, she told Savokġenaq to put some drops of hot water into the bowl while she mixed it in. Then, so it wouldn't dry out, she also put in a few drops of seal oil. After Savokġenaq gave her the water, she told him to stick two handfuls of the stinkweed into the hot water he had prepared and to keep it warm by the fire. With the paste in her hand, she went over to Kipmalook and talked to him, saying that she was going to put some of the medicine on his neck and chest.

"There, you will start getting better," she told him. Both Savokġenaq and Keenaq gave little sighs of relief. "You just rest now and don't worry about anything," Qutuuq said.

"Savokġenaq, take the rocks out of the pot, wipe them off, and put them on the fire again. We'll let the broth get stronger from the stinkweed and cool off before we give it to Papa," she said.

Qutuuq and Keenaq sat and talked to Kipmalook. "We're glad that you made it home," said Qutuuq. "You used all your strength to come home."

Kipmalook slept off and on fitfully. Qutuuq told him that she would be making something for his fever but that it would take a little while because Savokġenaq had to heat the rocks again.

She then said to her children, "Papa will get better. After you help me with the fever medicine, I think you two should go out and play." She remembered that she had wanted to let the children play more.

While she sat there by her husband, Qutuuq peeled off the willow bark. When Savokġenaq told her that the rocks were hot, she poured some water into another birch pot and placed the willow into the pot. To make sure she made the medicine strong, she put the bark that she had peeled off the willow into the pot, too, so that the medicine would surely bring down his fever. By that time, the stinkweed concoction had cooled enough for Kipmalook to drink.

Then Qutuuq said to Savokġenaq, "You go on the other side of Papa and help me lift him up a little. We'll try to get him to swallow a whole bowl of it so that it can help him with everything. It will give him some things that food and water give him and also make him feel stronger."

"Kipmalook, try to drink this medicine," Qutuuq told him after they had pulled him into a sitting position. He could barely open his eyes and drink. They held him up for what seemed like a long time, trying to make him finish one whole bowl full.

After they finished struggling to get the medicine into Kipmalook, Qutuuq told Savokġenaq and Keenaq to go on outside. They went reluctantly because they felt that they should stay with their mother and help her some more. But they knew that they had to do what she asked them to do. "You two go out and play," she said. "When we went on the river today, it was safe. Go down to that little slope near the edge of the river and slide down. Savokġenaq, you can get two furs from the cache and use them to slide down on. Not the big furs, but maybe the ones that are still stiff. They will make good sleds."

When the children went outside, Qutuuq stoked the fire and checked the fever medicine to make sure that all the bark and the willow were in the hot water. Then she went back over to Kipmalook and checked his feet to make sure that they were dry. She did not want him to catch a bad cold and get worse on top of what was wrong with his neck. Once more, she felt the lump that was under the skin. She couldn't feel where it stopped on the inside. It could be growing bigger where they couldn't see it or feel it. But the medicine should help. It always worked whenever they used it for aches and pains or cuts.

While the fever medicine was steeping, Qutuuq got out a rag made from worn-out squirrel-skin clothes. Those were the best to use for rags because all the hair was off and the skin was soft. She used this for a long time to cool Kipmalook down.

As she kept the rag on his head, she talked to him. "Kipmalook, you have to try to get well. We still have lots to do. We have to finish working on the skins, and you have to make one or two more trips to collect your traps."

By this time she thought that if she were assertive, he would listen. After she said that, she looked at him and noticed that he was sleeping hard. Then she said, "Go ahead and rest, and in a little while I will give you the fever medicine."

Qutuuq sat there. Then she looked over toward the place by the bed where she kept her personal items, went over and got out her blue earrings, and returned to the bed and sat down by her husband. She held the earrings in her hands, sometimes squeezing and holding them in one hand and then putting them in the other hand and holding them close to her heart.

"I inherited these blue earrings because my father was a great hunter," she said. "They mean that you can have a good life because you can provide everything. When I married you, I felt that I was still worthy of owning them because you are a great hunter. Kipmalook, you must get well. Please, get well."

She hoped that he had heard her, but it was okay if he didn't, because she wanted him to rest. When she said those words, they gave her the determination and strength to try and make him well.

It was time for Qutuuq to check on her children. She got up and told her husband where she was going just in case he could hear her. Once outside, she could hear the children over by the river where she told them to be. She walked over and was grateful to see that they were playing happily.

Savokġenaq and Keenaq wanted to show her how good the skins were working as sleds, so she told them that she would watch for a while. As she sat there and watched, they eventually made her smile because they were enjoying the sliding so much. She found that watching them made her relax a bit and she was thankful for that.

Before she left them, she said, "I'm going to get some dry meat from the cache for dinner. Play for a while and then it will be time to come in and eat. Savokġenaq, you're in charge." She noticed that he just shook his head to say yes, and then she started back to the food cache.

Qutuuq walked more slowly as she was becoming fuller in her pregnancy. And when she climbed the short willow ladder, went into the cache, and sat down on the floor, leaning against the skins, she found that she was out of breath. "Today was just too hard," she thought to herself. She checked her supply of dried moose and figured that it would last about a week. Then she checked her supply of seal oil and serra. She noticed that she had a few dried fish left and there was no more white muktuk. During the two months that Kipmalook had been working the trapline, it was his favorite food to take along because he felt that it kept him warm, so there was none left except for a few pieces of blubber, which is not the main part of the muktuk.

"Okay, don't panic," Qutuuq told herself. "I will make Kipmalook well, and before we run out of food, he will be out hunting again. But I'll start right now to ration the food. Also, we'll eat a late breakfast and a late dinner, only two meals a day. That should make the food last longer."

Qutuuq took some dried meat and the last of the seal oil and serra and headed back to the little sod house. The seal oil and serra were left out in the entry-way in the place where she kept foods that were to be eaten in the next few days. She placed them in a large wooden bowl that was there. To her that wooden bowl meant security. Usually she placed the leftover fresh meat that Kipmalook brought home from his trips there, ready for use the next day. Now she had no fresh meat, for her man was unable to hunt.

Back inside the little sod house, Qutuuq checked the willow-bark fever medicine and decided that the color was right. She readied some in a small birch bowl to give to her sick husband.

Sitting beside Kipmalook, Qutuuq said, "You have to sit up a little to take the fever medicine. It's ready now, so please try to wake up for a while."

Although Kipmalook's eyes were closed, she forced him to sit partway up and said loudly to him again that he must drink. He barely opened his eyes. She knew that he was drugged from the stinkweed, which should be relieving some of the pain he might be having. He listened and drank all the liquid. Qutuuq gave him only half a bowl full because the willow broth was stronger than the stinkweed solution. "There, your fever should start to go away," she told him. "You should relieve yourself while I hold a container for you while you're awake. I made you drink lots of fluids for your own good."

By the time Qutuuq was through, the children came into the sod house. She noticed that they came in quietly, not in their usual boisterous way. They both took off their parkas and quietly sat down. Qutuuq told them that Papa was sleeping very hard and that they shouldn't bother him. They acknowledged what she said and then told her how much fun they had had sliding down with the skins. Savokġenaq told her that they had built a little hill out of snow at the bottom of the slope so that they had a little jump. She smiled at them and said she was happy that they had had so much fun.

"After dinner," said Qutuuq, "we'll do our evening chores and go to bed early because we'll have to watch Papa during the night. I'll have to give him some medicine at least once in the night and again early in the morning. Tomorrow, after you've done your morning chores, you two can go sliding again."

In the middle of the night, Qutuuq found herself wide awake. She noticed how everyone else was sound asleep. No one made a sound. The wick on the oil lamp was barely lit. She decided that she would give Kipmalook the fever medicine and wait until the next day to give him the stinkweed solution again. She would also change the paste that she put on the lump just once a day.

When the willow medicine was ready, she went to her husband and lifted him up, talking in a quiet voice so the children wouldn't be disturbed. "Wake up for a while and drink this medicine again. Your fever is down. This will help keep it down."

Kipmalook made a sound that told her, yes, he would drink it. But he uttered nothing else. Qutuuq laid him back down and wiped his lips and chin. The blankets felt damp, so she knew that he was still feverish, and he felt warm too. There was a spare fur blanket by the wall, so she exchanged the damp blanket for the dry one. Qutuuq sat there for a while and then decided she better get back to sleep so she would have the energy to nurse her husband again the next day.

Utuktak's Visit

⁄⁄⁄⁄⁄⁄⁄⁄⁄

The next morning Kipmalook began to wake up, and it startled Qutuuq. She sat up quickly, wondering what he was doing. He didn't seem drugged like he had the day before.

He asked her, "How long have I been home?"

She told him that he had come home the day before and that he had been very sick.

"I couldn't check the traps," he told her.

"I know that. You got sick the night you left and then just brought yourself home. We're happy that you did because you might not have made it home. Do you feel hungry?" asked Qutuuq.

"No, but I need to get up and stretch and maybe walk outside a bit."

"Here's your parka. I'll help you," Qutuuq told him. She helped him do everything because he was weak and shaky.

Kipmalook grabbed her to get up while she put her arm under his arm. Slowly, he stood up and then had to rest a minute. Finally he said he could try to go outside but that he needed her support.

They were outside for only a short time before Kipmalook wanted to return to the little sod house. Kipmalook told Qutuuq that he needed to lie back down. She told him not to go to sleep because she needed to give him the medicines.

After lighting the fire and putting on the rocks to heat, Qutuuq gave him the fever medicine first. When she checked the birch pot, she realized she would have to make some every day for a while. While he was drinking the liquid, she asked him, "Does that lump on your neck hurt?"

He told her that it didn't hurt but that he was having trouble swallowing. She told him to take his time drinking the medicine and that he had taken it twice since yesterday and it seemed to be helping him. Then she told him about fixing the stinkweed solution that had drugged him all day. He said that he wanted to try to stay awake today but that she could put the paste on again.

When Kipmalook was through with the fever medicine, he lowered his head and said, "I'm going to get well. With your help, I know I will. Don't worry. I know that you are worried. With all the medicine that you are giving me, I know that you will make me well."

After applying the paste, Qutuuq went about making the morning tea. She felt that they were both anxious and worried and hoped that this would help some. Although Kipmalook was very ill, he was trying not to be, and she was aware of that.

They were so far away from the village that there was no way to go and get help. Qutuuq would have to leave her husband alone for too long a time, and there were the children to consider. As she sat down by Kipmalook to help him drink the tea, she said, "Here, this tea will help both of us. We'll share it like we share everything."

When she said that, she noticed that he had a weak smile. It was her attempt to humor him a little and to relieve their worries for the moment. Kipmalook reached over and gave her arm a squeeze and thanked her for everything. She smiled back at him and gave him more tea.

While Kipmalook rested and then slept again, Qutuuq sat by her oil lamp. She always felt a sense of security when she sat by her lamp. The flame was always strong; it never went out from people going in and out the door.

It was quiet in the little sod house. When Qutuuq checked the children, they were still sound asleep; so she pulled a skin up for a pillow and lay down too.

While she was sleeping, Qutuuq dreamed about her mother. They were out on the tundra picking salmonberries and had been talking about sewing the rain gear the winter before. It was raining, and they both had on rain gear made from ugruk intestines. She liked the sound of the rain hitting her raincoat while she looked at the salmonberries at the next area where she would be picking. Just before she woke up, her mother had been smiling at her because they were so happy to see all the salmonberries.

Awake now, Qutuuq heard something. It couldn't be her mother coming into the sod house—they were many days up the river by boat—but it sounded like someone was coming in. She quickly checked to see if it was Savokǵenaq. Maybe he got up and went to use the outhouse. No, it wasn't any of her little family. They all were still asleep in their beds on the floor.

Qutuuq had not gotten up but was propped on her elbow watching with sleepy eyes to see who— or what—was coming into the sod house. Her heart started to pound. She was so afraid that she couldn't wake Kipmalook, although he was too sick to help and should not have been disturbed anyway. So she waited to see who it was.

Suddenly that person was inside. It was dark except for the glow of her oil lamp. Then the person said, "I heard that Kipmalook was sick, so I came to see if I could help."

Qutuuq recognized the voice. It was Kipmalook's mother, Utuktak. Before Qutuuq could say anything, her mother-in-law said, "When I get back to the village, I will send some help."

As she was talking, the glow from the lamp hit Utuktak's face briefly, and Qutuuq could see that it was really her. "Don't bother to get up because I have to go right back," she continued. While she was saying this, she went over to her son, put her hand on his neck, and then walked back toward the door and was gone.

Qutuuq got up, rubbed her eyes, and then sat back down. She told herself that Kipmalook's mother really had come to visit them. She was awake. It wasn't her own mother. Her mother had been in her dream. This person who came in was Utuktak.

"I wonder why she didn't stay longer so that everyone would know she was here?" Qutuuq said to herself. She tried to remember everything that had happened. Finally, she decided if Kipmalook's mother had indeed come, then she should be glad that she would be sending help.

"I better get busy and make more medicine," she thought. This was the best time to work on it, while everyone was still asleep. She got up, put on her warm parka, and quietly went outside. It was freezing cold when she went out. She could feel how cold it was when the wind hit her face. It was still dark, but she tried to look for footprints anyway. "I will look for Utuktak's footprints when it gets light, and I won't say anything because I could have been dreaming," she thought to herself.

Once again, Qutuuq walked to the food cache. As she was walking there, she could hear her feet crunching the frozen snow. Occasionally, the wind made a sound coming through the open space by the river. When she went into the cache, she knew exactly where the medicine was and how much to get because she had sorted it all out the day before. She also knew where the dried meat was and how much to bring in. When she got to the door of the little cache, she sat there and started to cry. "I hope someone will come and help us," she said to herself.

When she got back to the sod house, she put the stinkweed, willow, and dried meat down neatly on her work space. She tried to work quietly so that her family would stay asleep. She had the two medicines soaking in water, and she could smell the stinkweed. Today she would give her husband more of this to make him sleep all day, even though he wanted to do without it.

Once again, there was nothing else for Qutuuq to do but lie down and wait until her children woke up. So she lay down on her daytime place right by her work space.

This time she dreamed of helping her mother cut salmon for drying at their summer camp. Both her parents threw out the little net and pulled in the fish together, and there were lots of red fish hanging on the fish racks. She could see her mother sitting on the ground at the river cutting fish while her papa washed them in the river and hung them. This place in her dream was nice and warm with a slight summer breeze, and she could see the same kind of low mountains as the ones they were at right now. While she was enjoying the mountain scenery in her dream, Savokġenaq woke her.

"Wake up, wake up, Mama! You're having a bad dream," he was saying to her.

"It's okay, Savokġenaq. It was a good dream," she told him.

As Savokġenaq was getting ready to go outside, Qutuuq said that she would go with him. Normally, he would go by himself and do the things his father always did several times each day: check the weather, look around for animals, and make sure nothing was disturbing the cache. When they got outside, Qutuuq watched Savokġenaq till he finished. He wondered why his mother was just standing there by the entryway.

When he went by her, he asked, "What's the matter, Mama?"

She sat him down on the ground, facing her, and held his hands. She told him about how she had seen Utuktak, his grandmother, come into the house and tell her that she would send some help from the village. But now she wasn't sure if she had been dreaming, because she was having lots of dreams since his papa got sick. "We should look on the ground and see if we can see her tracks," Qutuuq said.

Savokġenaq remembered what his shaman grandparents did when they were trying to pass him their powers. "Did she have on white-soled mukluks?" he asked his mother. "Because if she had those on, we won't find any tracks."

In her mind, Qutuuq tried to picture again what had happened. She was propped up on one elbow as she watched Utuktak come into the sod house. Qutuuq wrinkled her face and tried to picture what was on her feet. From her other dream, she could hear the raindrops on her rain gear. What that sound really was, though, was Utuktak's mukluks as she came into the sod house. Now Qutuuq could see the white-soled mukluks. She opened her eyes, looked at Savokġenaq, and said, "Yes, she did have her shaman boots on."

"Then that's how she got over here," Savokġenaq said. "I've seen Grandpa go somewhere. He says that he's gone to the moon and back because his white soles turn green. That's what he tells whoever is in their place when he is doing that. Grandma probably knew that Papa was sick and wanted to come and see for herself."

"We'll keep this between you and me, Savokġenaq," Qutuuq said.

They got up and walked back into the sod house. Keenaq was still asleep, so they just lay back down. This time Qutuuq didn't go back to sleep, but she told Savokġenaq to. She thought about what Savokġenaq had said. If that was what Kipmalook's parents could do, she was glad that they weren't living in the same village with them. "I wonder if his grandparents did pass some of their power to Savokġenaq," she thought. "If they did, I'll make sure that he doesn't practice it, because I do not want my child to live that kind of life when he grows up."

That day Qutuuq convinced Kipmalook that he should have some of the stinkweed medicine and sleep another day. He always just touched the top of her wrist to say yes, and she knew what that meant. Although he had wanted to stay awake that day, he knew that something was terribly wrong where he swallowed and was glad that he would be sleeping.

Before the children went out to play, they ate and finished their morning chores. Since the river ice was fully frozen and safe to go out on, they could now use it for water instead of melting snow. They used a pick to chip the ice. All three of them worked at this chore. As Qutuuq chipped the ice, the rhythm of the chipping made her sing the rock-juggling song to her children. Savokġenaq seemed shy about singing along, but he listened. Keenaq tried to sing with her mother. Qutuuq listened to the sound of Keenaq's voice and was pleased that she could sing so well.

Watching and Waiting

//////////

As the days went by, Savokġenaq noticed that they ate the same thing—dried meat and tea—for every meal. He asked his mother if he could go check the traps. Although he almost convinced her that he could do it, she used her better judgment and told him that he was too young to go out there by himself, that this was just the beginning of his training. Qutuuq did wonder if there was any whitefish left where they had buried some to age. Every time Kipmalook went down the river, he would bring some back. She counted about how many times he had done that and realized that the fish probably were all gone.

It was getting harder and harder to keep the family going. The food supply was slowly diminishing. By the time they were down to having one meal a day, Qutuuq made sure that they drank a warm tea for the first meal and then ate late in the afternoon so that they wouldn't go to bed so hungry. She still brewed the medicine day after day, so everything in the little sod house smelled like stinkweed and willow. Eventually, the children gave up going out to slide on the riverbank because they no longer had the energy. They, too, just did the minimal activity of bringing in wood for the fire, and they also followed their mother out to chip ice for water.

By this time, Qutuuq realized that Kipmalook was not going to get well. He couldn't talk anymore and just nodded his head once in a while. Most of the time, she kept him asleep with the stinkweed solution, but it always took a long time to get him to keep swallowing it. As she felt the large lump on his neck, she wondered what it was. It was something that she had not seen before. No relative of hers had ever died from this. She knew that it kept Kipmalook from eating, so he probably was starving to death. It was no use to try to feed him food anymore. He couldn't swallow it. After the children were asleep, Qutuuq sat by her husband and cried night after night. For their sake, she must be strong. But when she was alone, it was easy to feel scared and cry.

When the family went to bed now there was no longer a glow from the oil lamp because the oil was gone. There were only the red coals of the alder willow in the fireplace outside. Once in a while, even the coals seem to go black. There was no more laughter, no more smiles, and no more noise. Qutuuq realized that all three of them were hardly talking, just watching. Watching and waiting for Kipmalook to breathe his last breath.

One night, as the family sat in the little sod house, Qutuuq started to speak. She spoke to no one in particular and expected no answer. "I don't know how long it's been since Papa became sick. It must have been as long as the time we spent trapping and working on the skins—two full moons. Only the medicines and the tea have kept him alive for the last few days, and it looks like that's not enough to make him well. But this night and tomorrow, I will keep trying. We won't give up because that is how Papa is. 'Never give up,' he always says."

When she finished talking, she sighed and realized just how exhausted she was. "Utuktak said that she was going to send some help," she said, looking at Savokġenaq. "Maybe no one could come up this far right now or maybe they are sick themselves." She realized that maybe her own parents didn't know what was happening, even if other villagers did. Her parents could have traveled to another village. They were expecting the little family to arrive back in the village after breakup and to bring their skin boat back down the river. "Let's lie down and go to sleep now," she told her children.

When Qutuuq woke up, she could hear a storm outside. Usually, she liked the sound of a blizzard because it gave them a chance to rest from whatever they were busy with. But it was especially being with Kipmalook at those times that she enjoyed. They would sit together and visit and tell stories to their children. But this morning, she did not welcome the storm. She had too much to do. She got up slowly and went out to light the fireplace.

When Qutuuq came back inside, she went to her husband and knelt beside him. The moment that she took his limp hand, she knew that he was gone. It had not been long. He still felt warm. The first thing she thought of was how he wouldn't have waked her even if he could. He wanted her to get all the rest that she could. He was thoughtful that way.

Qutuuq sat by Kipmalook, not wanting to believe that he was really gone. She had worked so hard to try to make him well. "What will I do now?" she kept repeating in her mind. Her thinking was not clear. She could not afford to cry out loud. She wanted her children to sleep all day, if they could, because there probably wasn't any food left. Later, she would go back to the cache to see if there was any more. While her husband was still warm, Qutuuq thought that she should lie down by him once more. She put her head by his head and put her left hand across his chest and went to sleep there.

When Qutuuq awoke, she got up and went outside. She walked against the wind toward the food cache. Once she had to stop and turn her face from the storm and rest. Her breath came loud, she thought, as loud as the storm that she was in. There were little drifts of snow where there hadn't been any before. At one point, she fell because she could not see the snow. When she fell, she could feel the baby move inside her. "I'm sorry," she told her baby. "I didn't mean to hurt you."

Finally, when she reached the food cache, she held on to it because she was feeling pain from the fall. She winced from the pain, but still she did not cry. "I have to be strong for my children," she told herself. When the pain lessened, she slowly climbed into the food cache and sat there to catch her breath. As her eyes tried to become accustomed to the dark, she kept wiping her face. She didn't know what she was feeling. She felt hot, but then she thought she was cold from the storm. She felt wet, but she knew that she had been wiping her face with her sleeve. At that moment, every-thing seemed unreal, but she knew that she had to keep going for her children's sake.

When she could finally see things in the dark, Qutuuq reached over to the spot where they usually kept the dried meat. Her hand stopped where she should have felt some, but there wasn't any, only the frozen willows of the floor. Then she checked all the cracks in the floor and in the corner of the little cache. No food. Up the wall a bit, her hand got caught on something. She pulled it free from the frozen wall and held it with both hands. It was a couple of strands of tundra tea. Now she cried. The sound was a sad wail. She cried hard because her children couldn't hear her now. "What will I do?" she kept saying. "He's gone, and now all the food is gone. What will I tell my children?"

Walking Back

/////////

Although Qutuuq knew that they must start back, leaving her husband behind was something she had never imagined doing. Everything they did involved teamwork between them. That was how they worked— from making the trip upriver in the Fall to building the sod house, preparing the foods, and planning the traplines. But now she had to finish the rest of this journey by herself, along with her two children.

Just before they started walking back downriver, Qutuuq checked the clothing that Savokġenaq and Keenaq had on. Although they wore the same items of clothing every day, she checked anyway. They all wore the two undergarments made of squirrel, as well as warm socks made of rabbit skin inside their everyday mukluks. All three had a parka as their outer layer of clothing, and the two children had outer pants made from moose skin. Qutuuq didn't fit into her outer pants because she was very large now in her pregnancy, so she threw hers in the bag with the furs. She was thankful that she had planned ahead and made herself the inner layers of clothing big enough to be comfortable. They all had fur mitts hanging from leather strings and tied behind their backs, should they need them later. In addition, Qutuuq and Savokġenaq would each carry one bag of fur, and between them they would take an ulu and six cooking stones because they still had some matches. They would carry the birch pot for heating water, and Savokġenaq would carry his papa's gun.

When Qutuuq was through checking everything, they all stood there. The two children were looking at their mother but not saying anything. She knew that she was forgetting something. Every time they went somewhere, she always seemed to forget one or two items, so she wanted to take her time before starting out.

Suddenly Qutuuq remembered her blue earrings. She had worked so hard to put together all of the things that would help them on their trip back to the village, but in her haste she had forgotten perhaps her most important material possession. Now she would have to crawl back inside the sod house one more time to find her earrings. She told her children to wait for her outside, and, with her breathing loud and labored and holding her huge stomach with one hand, she went back into the house. She looked around, trying to remember where she kept them, momentarily confused by the enormous turn of events in her life in the past few weeks. She remembered where to look and found her earrings in her place next to the bed. She untied her mittens and buried the blue earrings deep inside one of them for safekeeping.

Now she was anxious to leave. No more time to grieve; it was time to go.

"The earrings help me," Qutuuq said to herself. "Every time I think about them, they help me. Now I must gather my children and leave this place." She thought of her husband, at peace in the cache.

When she got back outside, she stood there looking at her children. Savokġenaq was holding on to the huge bag of furs, and the gun was in his left hand and leaning against the ground. Keenaq was not holding anything, so Qutuuq asked if she wanted to take her hand-game that Papa had made for her. Keenaq shook her head and told her mother that she would carry the birch pot.

Qutuuq said, "On our way back to the village, we can switch bags, if we need to, and help each other carry these few things that we need with us. Let's go now.

We'll go down to the river and follow it. That way, we won't get lost in the storm."

The winter morning sky was still dark and overcast with heavy, dark gray clouds, and it looked like it wouldn't get better. They could feel the ground snow swirling around them, as if it wanted to help them get moving.

Qutuuq couldn't believe how hard it was to take those first few steps, but she knew that to stay in the safety of the sod house meant they would starve, because there was no one to hunt. To go out in this weather with two small children, not knowing how long it would take them to walk down to the village, was a serious break in the rules of living in the cold country, but it was the only thing that she could do.

"We'll walk on this side of the river," Qutuuq told her children. "We'll take our time, and that way, we'll be able to walk farther."

Qutuuq knew that she must keep talking so that all three of them wouldn't be so afraid. The only other sound was that of the storm as it whistled through the mountains and down into the willows that lined the river.

When they had walked only about fifty feet, Qutuuq told her children to stop because of a sudden pain she was having. They all sat down, and she tried to lean on her big bag of furs, but couldn't because it wasn't high enough.

Qutuuq put her hand on the bottom of her stomach and tried to rub the pain away. Savokġenaq and Keenaq watched her face. They were both afraid, and Qutuuq knew that. She was their only parent now, and she must get them back to the village safely.

"Help me a bit, Savokġenaq," she said. "Just let me lie down on my side for a while and then we can walk again."

While she was lying on her side, Savokġenaq held Keenaq, and they both sat down on the frozen ground next to their mother. He didn't know what to do.

"It will be okay," said Qutuuq. "I just need to lie here for a while. Take care of your sister, Savokġenaq."

Keenaq and Savokġenaq watched their mother without moving. She touched both of them with one hand to reassure them, while trying to rub the pain away on her stomach with the other. It took about half an hour, but the pain finally subsided. Qutuuq told herself that anytime she felt a pain, she would lie down and make it go away, but they needed to keep walking.

When they started off again, Qutuuq reminded her children to walk slowly.

"If we walk slowly, our clothes will not get damp from our sweat and we will stay warm."

It was still stormy, and the wind was still whistling through the tall willows. The trees looked dark and made scary-looking shapes. Qutuuq asked Savokġenaq to lead them on the trapping trail that he had taken with Papa.

Savokġenaq looked around and tried to remember which way the trail was, but he was confused. Too many things had happened, and too much time had passed since they had walked the trail. He started to cry softly, and Qutuuq saw that.

"Don't cry, Savokġenaq," she said. "I was only trying to make conversation so that we could hear ourselves talk. I really don't expect you to know which way to go. What we'll do is walk on the ground on this side of the river. And when we have to, we'll walk on the river. We'll let the river be our guide, even in the dark, because it leads down to the village."

Savokġenaq acknowledged what his mother said with a nod of his head.

Already, it was becoming too hard to walk, because the storm had piled up fresh snowdrifts that were about two feet high and in some places higher than that. Qutuuq told the children to sit down for a while. "When it starts to get light, we will go down on the river. But, for now, we'll rest every few yards and try to walk through this snow." There was nothing showing on the ground. All the reindeer moss was covered. There were only bare willows with dead leaves blowing in the storm. Keenaq pointed to the east, where there was a sliver of light. All three of them turned their sitting position to the east and watched for a long time without saying anything.

Qutuuq thought about the little ceremonies that she would lead her family through when Kipmalook brought home animals, how they would thank those animals for giving them food. Then she started wondering who it was who had made that light. After a while, she realized Savokġenaq was talking to her.

"It looks bright enough now, Mama," he said. "Let's go down to the river and see if it's safe to walk on." He helped his mother get up from the ground.

Qutuuq felt that her body was relaxed from sitting there watching the sunrise. "It was good to rest," she thought to herself.

As they began walking again, they looked back and could still see their little sod house. How Qutuuq longed to go back where Kipmalook was. But she quickly pushed that thought from her mind. She must keep on walking for the children's sake. Savokġenaq did not want to die.

"I never asked Keenaq because she is too little. But if she could understand, I'm sure she would feel as Savokġenaq does," she thought to herself.

It was very hard carrying that big bag of furs. It mostly dragged on the ground. Every time Qutuuq noticed twigs on the frozen ground, Qutuuq lifted the bag a little so that it wouldn't tear. She watched Savokġenaq, who was up ahead with Keenaq, trying to carry the other bag of furs. In one hand was his papa's gun.

"Maybe he's carrying it for nothing," she thought.

Qutuuq promised herself that she wouldn't say anything to Savokġenaq about leaving the gun. "I think it makes him feel that he is the man of the family now. When he wants to leave it, that will be okay, too," she thought.

When the children reached the frozen river, Qutuuq told them to wait. They stopped at the edge and waited for their mother to catch up.

Savokġenaq tried to comfort his little sister. "Remember those skins that we used to slide down the bank of the river?" He looked at his sister's face, and she looked back at him with a little smile but didn't say anything. "When we get to the village, we will have Mama make us sleds and we'll go sliding again."

When they looked back to see how far off Qutuuq was, she looked like she did when she was having a pain earlier. Savokġenaq dropped his gun and ran back to her. Keenaq ran back also. When they reached her, she told them that she needed to stop again. Savokġenaq said, "That's okay. We'll sit by you." This time, Qutuuq asked him to rub her lower back, and Keenaq said, "Put your head on my legs, Mama."

As Savokġenaq rubbed her back, Qutuuq held her stomach with both hands and took deep, slow breaths. After a while, the pain stopped again, but it had made Qutuuq very tired. She told her children that she would like to rest there for a while longer.

Then Qutuuq asked Savokġenaq, "Is the river safe?"

He answered by telling her that he didn't see any water along the edges. She smiled weakly at him and said, "Just a while longer and we'll go down and walk on the frozen river. It should be easier than walking on the frozen tundra with all the snowdrifts." And she closed her eyes.

When Qutuuq opened her eyes again, she realized that she had taken a nap. She quickly looked around and saw that Savokġenaq and Keenaq had fallen asleep by her. She sat up and wondered how long they had been asleep because the storm had died down.

"Wake up, children," she said quietly. "It's time to go again." She was thankful that the storm was over because she had to take off Keenaq's outer parka so that the little girl could relieve herself before they started to walk.

When they got to the river's edge, Qutuuq scanned the river ice for any wild animals and carefully checked for any water. Although it was winter, sometimes when the temperature rose during a storm, it would cause an overflow on the river ice. This last storm didn't create one, and she was thankful because she had to take her family on the river.

The riverbank was not steep, and Qutuuq grabbed a willow branch and let herself down to the frozen river. Savokġenaq threw the two bags of furs down, and he and Keenaq slid down about three feet. He held on to the gun, holding it above his head.

Once they all were down on the river, they began slowly walking again. It was light enough to see the snowdrifts on the frozen river. If it had not been a sad time, the texture of the snow would have been perfect to play in. It was a dry, warm snow, the kind that a person can grab with both hands and fling up into the air and watch float down. It wasn't a whiteout kind of day because they were able to distinguish the difference between the newly fallen snow and the frozen ice of the river. It was quiet. The only sound was their footsteps.

It was getting to be late in the morning, the time they had switched to for their first meal. All three of them were starting to feel hungry.

Keenaq looked at her mother and asked, "Are we going to find something to eat?"

"Try not to think about food. Instead, try to remember how many curves in the river we will be walking around. Here's the first one," Qutuuq answered.

Then Qutuuq told her children to stop and pick up some snow to put in their mouths. They sat down on the river by a drift and started eating bottom-snow. Afterward, they still felt hungry. Qutuuq said, "We just have to keep walking."

Every time they went around a curve in the river they stopped and ate snow. Then Qutuuq remembered the water bag that she had made from an ugruk bladder.

"I knew I would forget something," she thought. "Anyway, counting the curves keeps us busy. I wish there was something more interesting for the children to count."

The distances between the curves on the river were long, and the view never changed. Every time they went around a curve—and they had reached the third one now—Qutuuq kept hoping they would see something different so that it would take their minds off how hungry they were getting. But it was the same white river, willows along both sides, no animals. It was as though the animals knew how afraid they were and stayed out of sight. Keenaq began to cry. Qutuuq told her that she was doing so well.

"Please don't cry," she told her daughter, and then she couldn't help it any longer. She stopped, put her bag down, and began crying also. She held her children, sat down on the snow with them, and they all cried.

They had become very hungry now, and Qutuuq was beginning to feel weak and shaky. It was also starting to get dark.

"We'll walk back up onto the same side of the river and make camp for the night," she told her children as she wiped their tears and her own. "We'll be okay now. We'll be okay," she said, trying to comfort the two children and herself.

The Baby

/////////

Slowly, they all got up, picked up the things they were carrying, and started toward the riverbank. Qutuuq looked around at the willows and decided that they needed to dig in under some thick bushes to try and keep warm and safe from wild animals. When she found the best spot, she told Savokġenaq and Keenaq to help her dig out the snow. It was still soft from the storm. She told Savokġenaq to pull out the skins from his bag and lay them on the ground. They used the skins from her bag for cover, weaving them into the willows about two feet off the ground.

As Qutuuq was placing the skins, she suddenly remembered that the willows they used for headaches, and that were all around them, were edible. At least we can chew on something, she thought to herself.

"Savokġenaq, see these willows here? Try to break off three of them and bring them to me," Qutuuq told him.

When Savokġenaq brought them to her, she sat down on the ground and started peeling off the bark. It was hard to do because they were so frozen. When she managed to peel about two inches off one, she handed it to Keenaq. "Chew on this, my little one," she told her. Keenaq reached for it and started to chew on the frozen willow. Then she did the same with Savokġenaq's and with hers.

As they chewed, they watched the sky grow dark. It was a clear night, not like the night before. There was no sound of wind or wild animals, only the sucking sound that the three of them were making trying to get the juice out of the frozen willow. After a while, the medicine seemed to have a calming effect, and they started to feel tired from having walked all day long on a path that looked the same everywhere.

When it came time to crawl into the little shelter they had made, Qutuuq told Savokġenaq to load his gun and to place it at the side where he would be sleeping. She wasn't sure if Savokġenaq knew how to do that, but he did. His papa must have taught him when she was busy doing other things. She was grateful that Kipmalook taught him how to use the gun.

Qutuuq knew that she should sleep in the middle so that both of the children would be touching her. It was hard for her to crawl into such a little space because she was so big. Savokġenaq helped her by pulling her in. When she finally got settled, her breathing was labored, and she told Savokġenaq that she had to turn on her side and that she would first turn toward Keenaq. He told her that he would turn the other way and he wasn't afraid. They quickly went to sleep, and surprisingly it was a very quiet night.

In the middle of the night, Qutuuq was suddenly awakened by an excruciating pain. Her left arm went quickly to her lower stomach to try to make the pain go away. By doing that, she thought that she could go back to sleep because they had kept warm in all those skins. She tried to lie still so that she wouldn't wake her children. Pretty soon, the pain did go away, and she did go back to sleep.

About an hour later, the same pain woke Qutuuq again. This time she sat up because the pain seemed to be stronger. It frightened her. Her face was creased with the pain. She tried to keep still and quiet, but she was taking deep breaths now. And this time she couldn't go back to sleep. Another fear was taking over, and this was added to her fear of starvation.

"I can't feed two children, what am I going to do with three?" she asked herself. "I'll lie here and see if the pain will stop. The baby isn't due for another month yet. If I hope hard enough, it might stop."

She turned toward Savokġenaq and lay back down on her other side now. Because she had such hope, she managed to get back to sleep.

While sleeping, Qutuuq dreamed that she was back in her little sod house visiting with Kipmalook. He was telling her about Savokġenaq, how proud he had been of his son when he took him on the one-day trapline. That Savokġenaq would be a great hunter someday because he really listened to his papa whenever he told him what to do. As she was smiling back at Kipmalook, she was suddenly awakened from her pleasant dream by the pain again.

Qutuuq sat up and began to take long breaths. The pain was stronger, and she struggled to think clearly.

"The baby is coming early. What am I going do?" She still did not want to believe that on top of everything else, this was happening. This time she knew that she could not go back to sleep. Breathing deeply, she could see her frozen breaths in the air.

There were wide gaps in their little fur shelter where one could see the outdoors. It was still the middle of the night or perhaps early morning. Like last night, before they went to sleep, there was still no sound out there. There were no animals making noises, no scratches in the snow or sounds of ptarmigan. It was just quiet. As Qutuuq thought about what she was going to do, she started to sob, still trying not to wake her children.

"Why is everything so hard?" she asked herself. "Why did Kipmalook have to die, and why are we still here trying to live?"

With that thought she quickly shook her head three times as if to say no to herself. She knew that Savokġenaq still wanted to live and that she would do anything for her children. She had to think what to do next. She knew that she could not go back to sleep this time.

"What do I normally do when I'm having a baby? When it's time, I go out on the tundra by myself. Why does it seem so hard this time? It shouldn't be any different." Then Qutuuq shook her head as if to say, yes, it was different, because her husband was dead, she was here with her two small children, and they all were starving to death. Qutuuq knew that she didn't feel as strong as she did before because there was no food. Suddenly another pain came. "Take deep breaths," she told herself. This pain was not as hard as the one that woke her, but she knew that she had to do something. She could feel the sweat now. It was easy to feel panicky, but she tried to keep still.

Then she thought of Savokġenaq, who was going to be a hunter. She looked at where he was sleeping. "If I have this baby near Savokġenaq, he will not be a good hunter. That is, if we live through this. I have to go away."

A long time ago, Qutuuq's mother had told her that a woman must not have a baby anywhere close to the men. That part of life was only for women, and if a man or a boy was exposed to birthing, it would take away his ability to be a good hunter. So, Qutuuq told herself that she must honor that belief even if the circumstances were not normal. She started to cry again.

This time Savokġenaq woke up. He asked her, "What's the matter, Mama?"

"I have to go away and have this baby, Savokġenaq," she answered. "Because of the problems we have had— the small amount of food, trying to leave Papa in a good place, trying to get us back to the village—all of this has made a difference in my body, and the baby is going to be early; it is going to be born today."

Savokġenaq quickly sat up, wiping his eyes, as if it would make him see better in the dark.

"Savokġenaq, you and Keenaq must stay here in this little shelter until I come back. Try to let your sister sleep all day except to go out to eat some snow or to relieve herself. You both will be hungry, so try to sleep all day.

I will come back as soon as I can. I will come back, Savokġenaq. You take care of your little sister," she told him, whispering so that Keenaq would not wake up.

Savokġenaq didn't say anything; he just nodded.

With that, Qutuuq slowly and quietly crawled out of the shelter, pulling along the skin that she had on top of her so she would have something to use when the baby was born. When she got outside, she tried to notice which direction the wind was coming from. There was only a hint of breeze, and it seemed to be coming from the east as it did most of the time. That meant she should go back up the river or across the river, so that the wind would not carry any of the birthing sounds back to the shelter where her children were. Rivers and water always frightened Qutuuq. She remembered that dream she had of Kipmalook being washed away, so she decided to walk back up the river that they had come down on, but she would remain on the same side as her children.

While Qutuuq was standing there, another pain came. It was a bad one. She had to crouch down on the ground. It was so hard that she forgot to breathe deeply and just started to cry softly. The pain lasted for about a minute. When it was gone, it was so hard for Qutuuq to begin walking. It was still dark out. The thought of wild animals went through her mind, but she told herself that they hadn't heard anything the day before, and, this morning, it was very quiet around them. Only the sound of her footsteps on the frozen snow could be heard.

The snow wasn't as soft as it had been when they had walked down from the sod house yesterday. It had a frozen crust on it that broke through wherever she walked, making it harder to travel.

As Qutuuq walked back up the river, she looked at the sky and knew that it wouldn't storm that day. She was thankful because she didn't want the children to be frightened by the wind while they were lying in their little shelter and she wouldn't have to deal with the wind while she was waiting. When she was almost to the first curve of the river, another pain came. This one made her fall down on the river ice. She remembered to breathe through her teeth and knew that she could now scream to ease some of the pain.

When that pain was over, she lay on the skin, opening and closing her eyes, brushing sweat off the top of her forehead and wiping it on her soft squirrel pants with the fur turned in.

Qutuuq lay there resting and trying to think. "If I can make it to the top of the riverbank, I will stay there," she thought to herself. So she forced herself to stand up. "Just walk up there; you will make it," she said. Once she got up, it seemed a little easier, but she was very weak. "I have to make it through this to bring my children to the village," she said out loud. As she dragged the skin on the frozen-crusted snow, the day was becoming a little brighter.

"Good," she thought, "I'll be able to see what's under the willows." When she took a step, she felt like she just wanted to stay there. Then she took another step and caught her breath. She told herself, "Keep walking." This time she took more than one step. On and on she walked up the river until she could climb up the riverbank. The willows were her handholds to pull herself up.

Standing under some high willows, Qutuuq stopped and tried not to breathe too hard. She listened for wild animals, but all she heard was the sound of dry leaves whispering ever so slightly from a soft breeze.

"It must be safe here. Anyway, I'm here now and I can't go anywhere else," she thought.

She put the skin down on the snow under the high willows. She lay down slowly on the skin and looked around. It was still not that bright out, so she couldn't tell if there was anything even a few yards from her. She could see about five feet around her, and there were no animals, just the curved lines of the willows.

As Qutuuq sat there waiting for another pain, she thought about this baby. She and Kipmalook had been so happy about the baby. They both loved children and spent all of their time and energy on raising Savokġenaq and Keenaq. Kipmalook had been training Savokġenaq to become a good hunter, and she was going to teach Keenaq how to put away food for the winter and sew clothes for the family. Both she and Kipmalook made sure their children knew how much they were loved.

Another pain was starting, and Qutuuq grabbed a twig and put it in her mouth so that she wouldn't forget to breathe fast and hard through her teeth. When it was over, she felt weak and hungry. She looked around as if she would find some greens somewhere. Instead, she found snow and grabbed a handful and ate it as if it were some kind of food. Then she lay on her side and used a willow root for a pillow.

"Why do you want to be born now?" she asked her unborn baby. "I can't feed you. I can't even feed my other two children. They are starving, as I am. Why are you coming now?" These were the thoughts in Qutuuq's mind. She lay there and cried harder than she had ever cried before.

She was surprised when another pain came; she must have been sleeping. Her body had become so exhausted from the trip from the little shelter to where she was that all she wanted to do was sleep. When the pain woke her, she felt weak and hungry and thirsty.

Qutuuq thought again about her baby. "Please don't be born now. I can't take care of you," she pleaded, but she knew in her mind and from her experience that she was just fooling herself.

She cried herself to sleep again and slept so long that it was daylight when she awoke. Now she didn't feel as tired as before. The little rest she was able to get had helped her, but she felt like her bowels were about to move.

Qutuuq pulled herself up with the help of a willow branch.

"I better take off my squirrel-skin pants first," she thought.

Slowly, she took off her mukluks and then her squirrel-skin pants. She still felt like it was all a bad dream.

"I can't do this. If I didn't tell Savokġenaq that I would be back, I could probably die here." She was feeling sorry for herself now.

It was so cold out, and it felt colder now that she had to undress. She crawled to the other side of her little shelter under the willows, about four feet away, and squatted down.

Qutuuq had thought that her bowels were going to move, but instead it was really the baby starting to be born. After she pushed for a couple of minutes, her water broke.

The next few minutes were a blur for Qutuuq. She crawled back to her fur. Suddenly, she didn't feel so cold anymore because she had worked so hard before and after her water broke. She used her soft pants as a towel to wipe the sweat from her forehead so that her face wouldn't get cold.

Qutuuq looked around at the willows. "I need help. Please help me!" she cried into the air.

Having cried out like that, she had startled herself and realized she had better use her experience because the baby was going to be born and she had only herself to depend on. She thought she had better lift herself up between two branches of the big willows. It felt better to have some support.

The pains were coming swiftly now. Every time Qutuuq had to push, she squatted down but used the willows to help hold herself up through each contraction.

The labor pains were soon about one minute apart, and it was hard for her to focus on any clear thoughts.

All she knew was that she was delivering a baby and there was no husband to help her when it was over.

The head was coming. She could see the dark head of a baby.

"Push, push," she told herself, and with one last push, the baby came all the way out and she caught the baby with gentle hands. The cord followed the baby.

She lowered herself back on to the skin and held the baby close to her face so that she could cut the cord with her teeth. When she raised the baby up, it began to cry. She wrapped it in her soft squirrel skin-pants and saw that it was a boy. When she saw that she had a son, she started to sob.

"Kipmalook would have been so proud of you," she said to the baby. She held him in her arms and wiped his face with the skin and licked his eyes clean and then wiped them again.

Qutuuq felt she had to push again, so she put her baby down on the fur skin and raised herself up between the willow branches and pushed. The placenta came out, so she pushed it aside and then held the baby again. A black cloud descended upon her as she realized what she was about to do.

"I love you so much, baby, but we are all dying. We all will starve to death or freeze. I can't let that happen to you," she said to her baby, there in the cold, under the tall willows, along the bank of the river road to their village.

Qutuuq kissed her new child, the second son of Kipmalook, then reached over and placed part of the placenta on the nose and mouth of the baby until his breathing stopped.

When she cried so long that there were no more tears, she wrapped the baby in her warm squirrel-skin pants, around and around, so that wild animals could not get to him. Then she made a hole in the snow under the willows. The hole went down to the frozen tundra, and she placed both the placenta and the baby in there, covered them over, and packed the snow down as hard as she could.

For a long time, Qutuuq sat on the bloody skin and mourned. It felt much worse than when her husband had died. She had done something that was against everything she held sacred, and she regretted it with all her being. But she remembered the stories the elders sometimes told of hard times when food was scarce and when people were starving, and how sometimes, when it was absolutely necessary, difficult decisions had to be made in order for the strongest to survive.

This baby is not suffering like we are, she thought. "I let you go only because I love you with all my heart.

I would not let you be born into this world only to starve because I have not eaten and can produce no food for you to drink. I will never forget you. I will think of you every day while I am alive," Qutuuq said to the mound of snow that she had made to bury the baby.

With those words, she stood up again and turned back toward the river to walk to her two children. It was early evening. She had been at this place since before dawn. Just as she was stepping off a little ledge to go back onto the river, her eyes caught something slightly covered with snow. She brushed the snow off and picked up some rabbit droppings.

"I have to make it back to Savokġenaq and Keenaq," Qutuuq said to herself as she slowly made herself walk. She stopped and rested every few feet, feeling as if she were walking in a fog. She did not want to believe what she had been forced to do to her newborn baby. Life decisions were hard and sometimes cruel because of the conditions under which she and her people lived. That is how far her thoughts would go every time she thought of what she had done.

"I must get back to Savokġenaq and Keenaq" was the thought that she tried to focus on. As she stumbled along, her bare legs stinging from the cold, it seemed to her that she had been gone a long time. She knew she felt like that because she had to go back on the same trail that they had traveled the day before. If she did not walk the same trail, she felt she might get lost because she was so disoriented by all she had gone through in the past twenty-four hours.

Rabbit Droppings

///////////

Finally, when her eyes focused on the little shelter, Qutuuq strained to see her children. They were not outside. Savokġenaq had listened to her and stayed under the furs with his little sister. Qutuuq thought about Kipmalook and thanked him for training Savokġenaq so well. He always listened to her when she told him what to do. As she kept walking toward the little shelter, she did not want to make much noise for fear of startling them if they were asleep. Sitting down to rest a few feet away from the shelter, she felt the rabbit droppings in her hands. "What should I do with these?" she asked herself. "Rabbits eat food. These droppings must be food." Then she thought of the cooking stones they had carried with them.

Soon Qutuuq walked over to the shelter and quietly lifted the fur that was hanging in the willows. Her children got up and went to her, and all three held one another without talking, their eyes brimming with tears. Savokġenaq and Keenaq were so happy that their mother was back.

After a while, Qutuuq told her children to go outside and find all the broken willows they could, that she was going to make a fire and melt some snow and make them nice and warm. They did what she asked them to do. While they were busy, Qutuuq looked for matches, the birch pot, and the cooking stones. She was so happy to see some life in her two children and now knew she had to make this broth from the rabbit droppings.

When the children brought her the willows, she said, "Now pick some strands of dry grass so that I won't waste these few matches." Then she told them to make a little circle with her so that there wouldn't be any wind. With all their fur parkas, this was easy to do. When her children's faces were so close to hers, it was easy to see the effect their situation was having on them. Their unkempt hair and dirty faces seemed to accentuate the fact that they were hungry. When the fire started to burn the grass, Qutuuq quickly added the skinny dried willows. They stayed close together to make sure that the willows began to burn. When they did, Qutuuq put on thicker willows. After the fire was burning well, they all sat nearby rubbing their hands together. The brightness from the fire accented the coming darkness.

"We will stay here in the shelter one more night," Qutuuq said to her children as she carefully placed the cooking stones on the part of the fire where it seemed to be burning strongest. "Here, Keenaq, go and fill this pot with snow from where you two did not relieve yourselves," said Qutuuq. With that comment, all three of them finally laughed.

It took about an hour to melt the snow a little at a time. Each time the rocks cooled off, Qutuuq took them out of the pot, dried them against her parka, and put them back on the fire, over and over again. When there was about an inch and a half of warm water ready, she put in a handful of rabbit droppings. She let them steep while the stones were heated one more time. Finally, the broth was hot.

"We'll drink the broth slowly because it is hot, said Qutuuq. "Here, blow on it like this," she instructed her children. Then she held the broth to Savokġenaq's mouth. It was their custom to give the best part of a soup to the hunter. Savokġenaq would soon be a hunter, and she naturally gave him the broth first. He blew first and then drank a little broth. While he was drinking,

Keenaq watched and was happy when it was her turn. The pot went around about three times, and then Qutuuq reached in and took a rabbit dropping and tried it first. It tasted like willows and had the consistency of nothing that she could compare it to. The children watched as she ate it. "Here, it's okay. Eat one, Savokġenaq. Maybe it will keep us alive," she told them. They ate them until they were all gone. There was a tiny bit of broth left, so she told them to take one more sip. It did make them feel better.

They sat together until the fire was almost burned out and just watched the sky. When they felt a slight breeze from the east, it was time to go to bed. As they snuggled by their mother, Keenaq said, "We're glad that you're back. When I got scared while you were away, Savokġenaq just told me to go to sleep, and I did." Qutuuq found Savokġenaq's hand, held it, and said, "I knew Savokġenaq would take care of you."

Then Savokġenaq asked, "Where's the baby?"

Qutuuq hesitated before answering, "The baby did not make it. He has gone to be with Papa." Qutuuq knew it was better just to say that for now. In time, when they could understand, perhaps she would tell them what really had happened. "Let's go to sleep because tomorrow we'll be on our way again," she said quietly.

It was still dark when Qutuuq awoke the next day. It sounded like the wind was blowing again. When Qutuuq went outside to check, she decided that they wouldn't be in a hurry to start. She would go back to sleep and get all the rest that she could.

Later, when they all got up, Qutuuq told her children that they would pack up the furs and begin walking again. Savokġenaq would help her put the furs in the bags, and Keenaq would sit and keep watch. Qutuuq knew that if she kept their minds off how hungry they were, it would be better for them. After filling the two bags with the furs, Qutuuq made sure that she put the rest of the rabbit droppings in the birch pot and the cooking stones in her bag just in case they would have to eat them again that day. When they were ready, Qutuuq asked Keenaq, "Did you see anything?"

"No, I didn't see anything," she replied.

"That's good. We should start now."

As they began to walk again, Qutuuq said, "Every time that we come to a bend in the river, we will sit and make a snowball from the bottom-snow and eat it." She remembered that seemed to work the first day when they started walking down the river. They could hear the wind blowing on their left side because it was coming from the east. Qutuuq wanted to believe that it was trying to help them carry along the bags of furs. Today she did not have to remind her children to walk slowly so that they would not get sweaty. Even if they wanted to, they couldn't, because they were too hungry and weak.

As they came to a bend in the river, they sat and made their snowball. As they were resting and eating the bottom-snow, Qutuuq told them again the story about the little boy who ate too much. When she was through, Keenaq said, "Our stomachs won't break open." And with a smile on his face, Savokġenaq shook his head in agreement. Qutuuq was happy that she was able to take their minds off their hunger again. When they were through eating the snowball, they started walking again.

The next stretch of the river was a long one, but Qutuuq encouraged the children to keep on walking. "Don't stop yet. Remember, we need to reach the next bend before we rest," she told them. As they were walking, she noticed that the clouds were moving toward the ocean. "Look at the clouds," she said. "They're also going where we're going."

As they walked, the scenery never changed. The river was lined with willows on both sides, and there were little hills sometimes on one side and sometimes on the other side. Only the clouds changed, and Qutuuq told herself to be thankful for that. At least they had something to watch while they were walking. "What does that cloud look like?" she asked her children. They both looked up at the sky. "It looks like a bear," Savokġenaq answered. "No, it looks like a mukluk," said Keenaq. And they all laughed. For the rest of that stretch in the river, the clouds entertained them.

While they rested at the second bend, eating a snowball, Qutuuq said, "We will walk one more stretch and then stop for the night. I took the rabbit droppings so that we can have them tonight." Savokġenaq and Keenaq kept eating the snowball without acknowledging what she had said.

"Let's walk again," Qutuuq announced. As they trudged slowly on the frozen river, she started to have doubts again about whether they could make it.

"Here Savokġenaq is carrying that gun, and we haven't seen any ptarmigan or rabbits he could shoot," she thought. "We're starving." She panicked inside.

Then Qutuuq looked at Savokġenaq and said, "Do you think you'll use that gun, Savokġenaq?"

He looked back at her and said, "I'm going to carry this gun because it belonged to Papa."

Now Qutuuq understood why Savokġenaq hadn't complained about carrying the gun along with the bag of furs. For him, the gun meant having everything to eat and having a warm home and being happy. Just what the blue-beaded earrings meant to her.

With that understanding, she said, "Okay, Savokġenaq. When you want me to help you carry it, just tell me. Now I can help you." He then handed her the gun to carry.

Food

It was getting late by the time they reached the third bend in the river, their destination that day. Qutuuq told her children to look for an easy bank to climb, that they would stop and make camp with the skins again. Since it was windy, she wanted to stop where the willows were thick.

When they found a good spot, Qutuuq said, "Pick up lots of dead willows and bring them to me." When they were done, she told them to find some dry grass to help start the fire. Because of the wind, they made the fire under some tall willows in a little clearing.

Keenaq said, "It's my job to fill the pot with snow." Qutuuq smiled at her, and then she and Savokġenaq watched as Keenaq filled the birch pot with snow. None of them wanted to eat rabbit droppings again, but no one complained. Qutuuq cooked with them the same way she had the day before.

When they were in their little shelter, Qutuuq lay down between her two children. "If we walk tomorrow like we did today," she thought, "maybe we will make it down to the village. We have made it for three days now." And with that thought, she closed her eyes.

It didn't take long for the three of them to fall asleep because of all the walking and feeling weak from lack of food. The wind was blowing hard in the middle of the night. The noise woke Qutuuq. She had to reach down and tuck the skin under her feet. For a minute, she listened to the sound of the blowing wind. She knew that it was snowing.

"We'll just stay put until the wind dies down," Qutuuq thought to herself. "I remember stories from Papa and Kipmalook about how it's always safer to stay in a shelter when there's a storm." So, with that plan, she curled up again.

That day, they got up only to go check the weather. It was good to crawl back under the furs and go back to sleep.

Late in the afternoon the blizzard stopped. Savokġenaq crawled out first and looked around. As he was standing about three feet from the shelter, he noticed a rabbit a short distance away, by some willows. He couldn't believe his eyes. He watched it without blinking. He slowly backed up toward the shelter without taking his eyes off the rabbit. He told his mother and sister to be very still and quiet because he saw a rabbit. They didn't move. Savokġenaq got the gun, which he kept on his side of the fur bed, and loaded it after pointing it toward the shelter's opening. Without making any noise, he went out again. A few seconds went by, and then the gun went off. Qutuuq and Keenaq raced to the opening, and when they looked out, Savokġenaq was already picking up the rabbit. He turned and smiled at his family.

Qutuuq told her children to gather some willows and dry grass to make a fire. They now knew exactly what to do without being told anymore. Savokġenaq started the fire with his little sister's help while Qutuuq worked on the rabbit. Keenaq knew that it was her job to get the snow melted. When they were done, they watched their mother. Without talking, she took some of the rabbit's precious blood and put some in her hungry children's mouths. Normally, they did not drink the blood, but it was nice and warm, and Qutuuq wanted to give them something while they waited until some meat was cooked. The rabbit meat was divided into four meals, including the one they would have that evening.

With her ulu, Qutuuq scraped and cleaned the inside of the rabbit fur because that would be used for storing the fresh meat. Now she knew that they weren't going to starve. They were going to make it unless they ran out of food again.

When the meat was done enough, Qutuuq said, "We want to thank this rabbit for our food tonight." Then she looked at Savokġenaq and said, "When a boy shoots his first animal, he is supposed to share it with an elder. When we get to the village, we will give the fur to my mother. She will be happy for that."

Savokġenaq nodded his head, trying to be respectful even with a hungry stomach. Then Qutuuq cut the meat and told them both to eat. The hot rabbit broth tasted the best because it warmed them all the way down to their stomachs. It was so good to eat real food.

"We will stay here again for the night," Qutuuq said. They waited for the fire to become red coals before they crawled back under the furs. When they were settled once more, she reached over to Savokġenaq and told him that he had saved their lives that day. She told him that he was truly a hunter now and that Papa would have been proud of him today. Savokġenaq was happy, and Keenaq even let out a little giggle, which made all three of them happy.

The next morning, when Qutuuq awoke, she listened to the wind. It had died down except for a whistle now and then. Before she woke her two children, she wanted a few minutes to herself. Surprisingly, she felt like she was starting to think more clearly now. She wasn't so sore from giving birth, and her body felt rested and a little stronger.

"I am thinking of you, my little baby," she thought to herself as she lay there. "I'm sorry that I did not let you live. I will feel this way for the rest of my life. Now I have to make sure that I bring Savokġenaq and Keenaq back to the village."

When she woke Savokġenaq and Keenaq, they, too, seemed stronger.

"We will try to walk a long way toward the village today. That means counting many bends of the river," she told them.

As they were packing up the bags, she told Keenaq, "Look both ways, up and down the river, and see if you see anything." When they were through putting the furs, cooking stones, ulu, and fresh rabbit meat in the bags, Qutuuq and Savokġenaq walked toward Keenaq.

She looked back at them and said, "I don't see anything. It is safe." When they first stepped down off the riverbank, they stepped into soft snow and sunk in almost to their waists. Qutuuq told them to crawl out of the holes they had sunk down into. Savokġenaq was the first one to stand up. When he did, he put his bag and gun down and pulled his mother and sister up.

"We won't hurry, but we'll walk very far today. That means taking shorter rest periods at the bends of the river," Qutuuq told her children.

As they walked, Qutuuq said, "Someday, you will have this story to tell your children. You will tell them how brave you were to have the will to walk all the way back to the village. How happy you were before Papa got sick and there was no one to hunt for us anymore. How much fun you had sliding on the riverbank and learning how to walk the trapline with Papa. Keenaq, at first you didn't do very much, but you learned a lot by watching. Then, on this trip, you were our snow gatherer and water maker. Papa would have been proud of both of you."

The children didn't answer, but Qutuuq knew that they had heard her and would remember.

"Look! Over there!" Savokġenaq was pointing down the river. They all stopped suddenly and looked. There were three foxes. Two were smaller and probably used to be the other fox's babies, but they were almost grown now. The foxes also stopped where they were. They were coming up the river, but they quickly let the people have the right-of-way. Qutuuq and her children dashed to the other side of the river, the side they never traveled on. They started walking again, and Keenaq said, "Three people, three foxes." And they laughed. It was good to see something different finally. It had happened so fast that no one became frightened.

Afterward Qutuuq said, "I just hope that they keep on going."

"Remember, I have this gun," Savokġenaq answered.

It had been a long bend in the river. As they sat down and ate some snow, Qutuuq reminded them, "We will take short rests today." Seeing the foxes had brought a little more life into the children. Their step didn't feel as heavy, not like the last time they were walking. It made them look around more to see if they could see anything else. Later on that day, they saw a flock of ptarmigan, but they were too far away for Savokġenaq to take a shot.

They could hear the ptarmigan calling, *Ka buk, ka buk.*

Qutuuq gleefully cried out, "Talk to us. Keep talking to us. We want to hear you. Tell us how far we have to walk. Don't go away!"

Then both children joined in. "Talk to us. Keep talking to us. We want to hear you. Tell us how far we have to walk. Don't go away!"

It sounded so good to hear one another that they repeated it again and again. They had mostly been walking in silence, so hearing other living things helped revive their spirits. Qutuuq felt once again that they were going to make it.

When they got to the last bend late in the day, Qutuuq was almost sure she could see the shoreline in the distance. The weather was still not very clear, but she wanted to believe that was what she was seeing. Also, it seemed like the hills were lower now. That meant that they had come down out of the foothills and should soon be reaching their little village on the Bering Sea.

Help

𝕀𝕀𝕀𝕀𝕀𝕀𝕀𝕀𝕀

Once again the little family looked for a good spot to build a shelter out of the furs they were carrying. Qutuuq wanted to make the shelter first so that they could go right to bed after they had eaten. She noticed that the willows here were not as tall. That was another sign that they were getting close to the village. They stuck the furs in the willows the same way that they had before. That had worked well. Savokġenaq made sure he put his gun near where he would be sleeping. Everything was routine now. Each knew what his or her job was. Qutuuq thought to herself, "My children are good people and quick to learn."

A while later, when they were through eating dinner, Qutuuq said, "There are some things that I want you both to know and understand. We live by rules, and that is why we can survive out here. First of all, we live by the rule of nature. That is, we respect the land and all the animals that live here. They help us by feeding us, clothing us, and sharing the land that we all live on. They have protected us with their spirits in the form of all our clothing— underclothes to keep us comfortable, a big parka to keep out the wind, mukluks and squirrel socks for our feet. It is the rule of nature to take just what you need, never to waste anything. If we are not greedy like the little boy in the tomcod story, we will have a lot all our lives. That is also the reason that each hunter shares the animal that is hunted and killed with the elders. Sometimes we will not have a lot to show, but if you are a good person, you have a lot. It will be in the form of happiness and a strong family to comfort and protect you. And then will come the respect of the people around you.

"Another rule that we live by is to have respect all of our lives for the elders. They are our grandmas and grandpas. They already have lived much of their lives, and because of that, we must listen to what they say and do what they say. They do not talk just for the sake of talking, but because they know something. Keep in mind that it will be hard to listen to them all the time, but someday, when you are older, you will understand what they were trying to tell you. I am telling you this because we are getting closer to the village, and when we arrive at the village, these furs will no longer belong to us."

For a long moment, Qutuuq just sat looking at the coals in the fire. She knew that her children would not question her because that is how she taught them. They were good children.

"There is a rule, made for us by our ancestors," Qutuuq continued, "that we must now respect. It says that when a son dies, whether he's married with children, or whether he's miles away, all of what he owns must be given to his parents. Now, here we are, and we must turn over everything that we have worked for. We cannot break any rules because, if we did, and then anything bad happened to the village, we would be blamed, and then no one would have anything to do with us. We don't want that. What we will do is go back and live with my parents and work for our living there. I know that my parents love me and will welcome us."

For a brief moment after his mother had finished talking, Savokġenaq wondered why he was working so hard carrying the furs back when they wouldn't belong to them when they arrived at the village. But he got ready for bed without questioning his mother. Keenaq was sleepy now and was happy to be going to bed in the little shelter.

The next day was clear and cold, so when they awoke, Qutuuq said they would eat first, before continuing on their journey. The hot rabbit broth was good and warmed their stomachs. While packing up, Savokġenaq remembered what his mother had said the night before. As he watched her, he thought she was thinking the same thoughts by the way she was handling the furs.

Qutuuq was really thinking of Kipmalook—how hard they had worked on the furs and the routine they had followed so that life would not be so hard. It was easy to do anything when you had a good partner. If one didn't know exactly what to do with a part of an animal, the other would remember. Because they had been so busy working on the skins, the days and nights had gone by fast. It was good to work hard, she thought. That's what she learned from her husband. And she told herself that she would take good care of her children because Kipmalook would have wanted it that way. She would not grieve for him anymore because it would interfere with the work that she had to do to raise Savokġenaq and Keenaq. She knew that her family would take part in teaching her children, but she was the one who would make sure of that.

As they came to the first bend in the river that morning, Qutuuq said, "Today, we won't stop at every bend. We'll stop at every second one. Is that all right with you two?"

The children both looked at her and nodded yes.

As they came to the second bend, Qutuuq pointed to the horizon. "See where the color changes? That's the ocean. It's still frozen, so it blends with the sky." Hearing that, Keenaq pleaded to walk faster. But Qutuuq said that they were still quite a way from the village and that they didn't want to sweat in their warm clothing.

"We still need to sit down and make a snowball to eat," Qutuuq said. While they were sitting there, she asked them, "What is the first thing that you will do when we reach the village?"

Both started thinking and didn't say anything for a while.

Then Savokġenaq said, "First, I will oil this gun and hang it up on the wall." He had a big smile on his face.

Keenaq said, "I will take all these warm clothes off." They all nodded in agreement.

While they were resting, Qutuuq began to worry about how she and her two children would be treated in her parents' home. She had told Savokġenaq and Keenaq that it would be okay to stay there because she didn't want them to be afraid. But it would be different for them. Her two children would probably be told what to do by other members of her family because everyone helped that way. This winter she had gotten so used to her and Kipmalook being the only ones to instruct them and tell them what to do. It was going to be hard to make that adjustment—for all of them.

It was time to walk two more bends of the river. Qutuuq wanted to keep to the walking schedule she had planned. She had become accustomed to living by a schedule. Since Kipmalook died, time had been in as much disarray as everything else. She told herself that she would begin building her life again, little by little, and sticking to her plan for the day was a good place to start.

At the next resting place, Qutuuq again wanted to talk seriously to her children. "When you were born, you were given the names of my grandparents who had died. My mother helped us name you. You were given the names of people who had respect from others, and so that is how your papa and I have tried to treat you. If you should ever do anything that dishonors those for whom you were named, their spirits would leave you because someone had to scold you. If their spirits were to leave you, life would be hard because there would be no spirit helping you. And if you behave badly toward others, it will begin to show on your body in crippling ways. It will make your body ache, and there will be nothing that will help you. You must have respect for yourself and then you can have it for others. It will hurt me if you do not behave, especially now, because we have no choice but to go back to the village and live with other people."

After saying those words, Qutuuq looked first at Savokġenaq.

He looked back at her and said, "Mama, I will try to treat others nicely all the time. And I will work hard."

Qutuuq answered, "Savokġenaq, you have always been a good boy, and I believe what you say. I just had to tell you these things because now we'll have to live with other people, and that will be hard for us."

Then she looked at Keenaq, who said, "Mama, I'm going to be nice to Savokġenaq, and I'll listen to him because he's the oldest."

Qutuuq smiled and said, "Now it's time to walk again."

They were anxious to reach the village, but they could walk only so far. They walked twice as far as usual, though, because they had energy from eating again. That night, they ate the last of the rabbit meat that Qutuuq had divided into little meals. When they made a fire, Qutuuq wondered if it could be seen from the village. She said to her children, "Let's hope that someone will see this fire and come meet us."

When they were arranging their skins in a little shelter, Savokġenaq was happy that they were using them before they were given to his grandparents. When he told his mother what he was thinking, she said, "It's okay to have those feelings, Savokġenaq. Just don't let those feelings make you do something that will get you into trouble."

Qutuuq hugged her children extra long that night before they went to bed. She felt that they needed to be hugged after she had to explain about the furs and how they were expected to behave when they got to the village.

The next morning, they all felt tired. "When will we get there?" Keenaq asked. Qutuuq told her, "Try to hold on a little longer. Maybe this will be over today." So they started to walk and this morning had nothing to eat again. Qutuuq wanted to reach the village that day.

"Because we don't have anything more to eat, we will keep going until we make it to the village," Qutuuq said to her children. "So today, when we walk, look for signs of people. Someone might be out hunting for ptarmigan or rabbit." Those words seemed to give Savokġenaq and Keenaq extra energy and strength. Their walk became more animated with the thought of finally reaching the village.

When they were at their second resting place, they looked in the distance, and their eyes widened. Coming around the bend of the river, about half a mile away, were two people. They both had their bow and arrows.

Qutuuq told her children, "Now, don't run. We'll wait for them here."

The children didn't run, since their mother had told them not to, but they couldn't help but yell and wave their arms. "We're here! Come here!"

They were so happy to see other people. The smiles on their faces were so big, and they grabbed one another's hands. With the smiles came a cry of relief from Qutuuq.

While she was crying, Qutuuq murmured, "Thank you, thank you, thank you." She was thinking of Kipmalook and the baby. In her mind, she told Kipmalook that she had brought their children home safely, and she told the baby that she would never forget him.

When the hunters reached them, Qutuuq saw that they were two of her cousins. One cousin said, "Last night someone saw your fire. We could barely see it in the distance. If you had made camp around the next bend up, it wouldn't have been seen. Everyone knew that your family was the only one up here this winter, so the village was alerted. It was decided that the two of us

would start out last night because we know the trails
and the river from hunting."

Qutuuq sat there and cried. When she was through,
she gave each of them a hug and said, "You don't know
how happy we were to see you come around that bend
in the river. For most of our journey, everything was the
same—same willows, same scenery—and there was not
much to hunt on this trail. We were warm enough, but
we are hungry."

Then the other cousin said, "Last night, before we
left, the women got some food ready. They thought
that you might be hungry. You can eat first, before we
make the trip down to the village." And having said
that, he put down his packsack and laid out the food in
front of them.

Qutuuq thanked the Great Maker for sending help
and food. When she was through, they all started to eat.
Food never tasted so good. The women had cut up some
dried ugruk dipped in oil with some blubber. They also
had sent some dried fish and serra. After that, they ate
akutuk made with blueberries and salmonberries.

While they were eating, the cousin Qutuuq was
closest to asked, "I don't want to be impolite, but what
happened to Kipmalook? You don't have to talk about it
if it's too hard."

Qutuuq answered, "No, it's all right. We've already grieved a lot, so I can talk about it. He died because he had been sick for a long time—about two moons. The medicines that I had could not heal him. He had a growth in his neck that got bigger and bigger, and then he became very sick and died."

The cousin became sad and didn't ask any more questions, though he had much that he wanted to ask.

When they had finished eating, the hunters packed up the leftover food and carried the two bags of furs that Savokġenaq and Qutuuq had been carrying. One of them said to Savokġenaq, "You want me to carry the gun?"

Savokġenaq shook his head and said that he could carry it. They knew that it had belonged to Kipmalook and now it belonged to Savokġenaq.

It took them the rest of the day to reach the village. After seeing their fire the night before, the villagers worried that something had happened to the little family that had gone upriver to trap, so they kept checking in at Qutuuq's parents' house to see if they had come home with the hunters.

When Qutuuq, her children, and her cousins finally arrived at the village, they began to hear the dogs barking. As they came to the first houses, Qutuuq held her blue earrings tightly in her right hand, trying to draw on their strength. She was physically tired from the long trip downriver and emotionally exhausted from the tremendous strain of losing some of her family while keeping the rest of her family alive. She thought to herself, "The next time I go anywhere, I will bring some dogs with me. That would have made it easier to come down the river. But I don't think that I will go anywhere for a long time now."

Once Qutuuq, Savokġenaq, and Keenaq arrived at her parents' home, they were made to feel very welcome. Icharaq and Anamiaq could not believe that their daughter and her two children had walked all the way back to the village. With the help of other relatives, Icharaq made sure the three travelers got comfortable, offering them clean clothing, food, and something hot to drink. Anamiaq made sure their home was warm and cozy by gathering plenty of wood.

While Qutuuq and her family were upriver at their winter camp, her parents had acquired a new item called a stove. They told her that people were starting to use stoves to cook food and to stay warm. You burned the wood inside it, and the smoke went out through the stovepipe. Qutuuq, Keenaq, and Savokġenaq kept holding their hands by the stove to feel the warmth. It felt so good.

As Qutuuq and her children settled in and rested, word was spreading in the village that Kipmalook had died at their winter camp. And as they rested, Qutuuq listened to the sounds of her mother visiting with the people who came by to check on Qutuuq and her children. Most people brought food. Some came just to offer their condolences and to see if there was anything they could do to help. Some of the elders would go over to Qutuuq because they were curious about how Kipmalook had died. In the next few days, Qutuuq told the story over and over. Despite her exhaustion, it comforted her that so many wanted to hear her story.

Epilogue

///////////

When Qutuuq and her two children were first helped to the village, they were taken to her parents' home. In the following days, while they were being cared for, one of the women of the village, Mulquay, came to them. She took Qutuuq, Savokġenaq, and Keenaq back to her home and told them they could live with her family for as long as they wanted. All three were still exhausted, dehydrated, and malnourished, but it was apparent how relieved Qutuuq was to have made it home. Her children stayed close to her, as they were shy around strangers.

Because of Mulquay's loving care, the survivors started to feel better. Qutuuq was too weak to tell anyone everything that she had been through. People knew that Kipmalook had died, but she could not bring herself to tell the whole story about her baby.

After a while, Mulquay thought that Qutuuq's children should be outside playing with the other children, but they didn't want to play. Savokġenaq and Keenaq knew that something was troubling their mother and would not leave her. Mulquay began to feel something more had gone terribly wrong while they were away from the village.

Thinking that Qutuuq was grieving for her husband, people outside the family left her alone, telling her that she and her children were safe now and that they understood why she was so sad. Perhaps it was this great concern for her that finally led Qutuuq to tell Mulquay what she had done with the baby.

Mulquay went to her husband, Salavialook (Steffan Ivanoff), for advice. They knew that killing girl babies was practiced by the Iñupiat at times, depending on the families and circumstances, but all boy babies were kept because they grew up to be providers. This woman they had taken in had killed a baby boy. The couple was concerned and went to get Qutuuq's parents.

When they were all together, Qutuuq was encouraged to tell the story of what happened on the river. It was important for the children to hear the story from their mother because they wouldn't leave her side and knew that something was burdening her.

After hearing the whole story and watching the terrible pain on Qutuuq's face, Qutuuq's relatives believed that she had truly felt there was no way to feed the baby or take care of him in the circumstances they were in. Icharaq told Qutuuq that people would be shocked by what she did, and some probably would look down on her. Even after hearing Qutuuq's story, Mulquay and Salavialook still wanted to help raise her children like their own and said that Qutuuq was more than welcome to live with them also. Qutuuq agreed, and the little family lived with Mulquay's family for thirteen years.

In time, Savokġenaq trained as a dog musher and worked as a mail carrier.

Mr. and Mrs. Axel E. Karlson, the first missionaries of the Covenant Church, gave Savokġenaq an English name—John—which he was called for the rest of his life. When Keenaq entered the church school, the missionaries gave her the name Emma. Qutuuq was given the name Ida, although she did not go to school.

Qutuuq and Keenaq helped with the household chores, and Qutuuq took on the job of seamstress for the family and worked with processing animal skins. Later, Keenaq became the fourth wife of John Kialook, and they named their son Kipmalook. All the three previous wives had died from tuberculosis.

In 1905, when the villagers went to spring camp between Chaqtuliq and Bonanza, Qutuuq met a man named Okitkun. He was from Kuuyuk, the next village north. When it became known that the two of them would like to be together, John and some other hunters brought them up to Haycock, upriver from Kuuyuk, where there was a marriage commissioner. Everyone in the family was happy for Qutuuq, and they all liked the man she married.

Okitkun was a reindeer herder. He owned the animals and provided very well for all the relatives. At the same time that he was caring for his reindeer herd, the couple ran a roadhouse, first at Kuuyuk, and then at Bonanza. Finally Qutuuq was no longer alone. She had a partner who helped her through good times and bad.

One of the good times was when John married a girl named Lily, whose Eskimo name was Tusalvik. Lily had gone to the Covenant Church School at Unalakleet and was preaching what she had learned about the Bible. She had been a classmate of John's sister, Keenaq.

John had always felt that there was a shaman's spirit around him until his second child was born. After talking with Lily about it, they both prayed and the spirit left him alone. He didn't fully convert to Christianity until his son, Fred, was born. Throughout his life with Lily, John took it upon himself to be her helper and would move them from place to place wherever she wanted to go and preach the gospel.

Qutuuq learned to pray for forgiveness through Lily, and this helped her deal with her guilt about what she had been forced to do upriver so many years earlier.

For Qutuuq, one of the difficult times was when she lost her daughter, Keenaq, who died from tuberculosis when she was still a young woman. Qutuuq took care of her grandson, little Kipmalook, after Keenaq's death, but he, too, eventually became ill and died of the same disease. So did Keenaq's husband. This time, Qutuuq did not have to go through her pain alone. She had Okitkun, John, and Lily.

Throughout the seventeen years that she and Okitkun had together, Qutuuq was always grateful that she could live a full life. Marrying Okitkun had given her status in the village again. She was not looked down on, nor did people feel sorry for her as they would have if she had no husband. She also put her hands to good use by becoming an excellent seamstress and even volunteered those services to help others.

One day in 1919, John's wife, Lily, visited the store in Kotzebue to pay the grocery bill. The man there was unable to find the bill under John's last name, Kipmalook. Lily noticed that the bill was under John Lily, so she decided to solve the problem by adapting John's Eskimo name of Savokġenaq for a surname. From then on, they were the John Savok [SA-vuk] family, and his descendants were given Savok for their last name.

After Okitkun passed away from old age, Qutuuq moved north to Buckland, where John and his family were living, and there she lived twelve more years helping in her son's household.

Some of her grandchildren still remember Qutuuq because she always made them new parkas or mukluks and made them feel special. While Qutuuq lived at Buckland, five new grandchildren were born to John and Lily Savok. James, Ida, Ruth, and Anna were already there, and after Qutuuq's arrival, Fred, Lydia, Joshua, Rachel, and Irene were born.

Qutuuq had the respect of her family and friends when she passed away in 1934, but always carried with her the guilt over her baby's death. Lily was with her when she died, and she said in Qutuuq's Native language, "Now, Qutuuq will be with her baby."

It was known that her last words were a prayer for forgiveness.

Generations

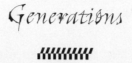

Date unknown–Koyuk, Alaska mom STORY about

Qutuuq as an elder with a tattooed chin like other
Iñupiat women of her generation. [PHOTO COURTESY

AMELIA NAGARAK LOVELL AND ELLIOTT BRADLEY]

215

1907–Unalakleet, Alaska

*Ķeenaq and Savoķgenaq
grew to adulthood and
were given English first
names by the missionaries
of the Friends Church.
Ķeenaq was called
Emma; Savoķgenaq
was John.* [PHOTO COURTESY
RUTH OUTWATER]

1915
her daughter
Keenaq (Emma) married John Kialook, and they named their son

Kipmalook, after Keenaq's father. All three members of the young family

would die of tuberculosis. [PHOTO COURTESY RUTH OUTWATER]

1920–Kotzebue, Alaska

son

Savokǧenaq (John) married Lily Egak and they began a family. Nearly obscured at center is their son, James. At front left is Ida, and the youngest is Ruth, the author's mother. [Photo courtesy Ruth Outwater]

1929–Buckland, Alaska

Back row, from left: James, Lily (packing baby Rachel on her back), and John. Front row, from left: Lydia, Fred, Anna, Ida (holding hands with Joshua), and Ruth. When the family's grocery bill was filed incorrectly because of name confusion, Lily decided to truncate her husband's Eskimo name to create a new family surname: Savok. [PHOTO COURTESY FRED SAVOK]

1947–Deering, Alaska

son

~~John~~ and Lily with their daughter Ruth (Savok) Outwater and two of

her children. At right is Theresa and at center is Loretta, the author.

[PHOTO COURTESY LORETTA OUTWATER COX]

1948–Nome, Alaska

John and Lily Savok [PHOTO COURTESY LORETTA OUTWATER COX]

2002–Fairbanks, Alaska

Ruth Outwater (top left) with daughter Loretta Outwater Cox and two of Loretta's daughters, Yolanda White, left, and Katherine Cox. At center is Yolanda's daughter and Qutuuq's great-great-great granddaughter, Sydney White. [Photo © Roy Corral]